BELFAST
AN ILLUSTRATED ARCHITECTURAL GUIDE

Belfast
An Illustrated Architectural Guide

PAUL LARMOUR

FRIAR'S BUSH PRESS
1987

To LYNNE, JANE and KATIE

Published with the assistance of the Esme Mitchell Trust and the Ulster Bank.

The Friar's Bush Press
24 College Park Avenue
Belfast BT7 1LR
Published 1987
© Copyright reserved
ISBN 0 946872 10 4

Cover design – Spring Graphics, Saintfield.
Typesetting – Textflow Services Ltd., Belfast.
Printing – W. & G. Baird Ltd., Antrim.

Frontispiece: City Hall: front pediment, porte-cochere, and statue of Queen Victoria.

CONTENTS

LIST OF COLOUR PLATES

Introduction

Belfast is a comparatively young city, and has no buildings of antiquity to grace it as have so many historic towns in Ireland. There is no ancient castle or cathedral at its heart; nor has it any of that great wealth of eighteenth century architecture that distinguishes other places. It has, however, a very fine series of buildings of the past two hundred years which reflect its remarkable rise from an unimportant provincial market town to a very large city whose change of fortune was based on industrial and commercial success.

It is true there are early references to Belfast, or Bealfearst as it was originally known (its name derived from *bel* or *beal*, meaning a mouth, and *fearsat*, a sandbank) but it appears to have been a fairly insignificant place until the early 17th century. In 1603 Sir Arthur Chichester from Devonshire received a large grant of lands in Ulster, including Belfast itself. The date of that grant is really the date of the foundation of the town. During his administration Chichester built himself a large mansion, in 1611, and two years later in 1613, on his advice, the town was constituted a Corporation by charter of King James I. Truly, Sir Arthur Chichester was the founder of modern Belfast, although nothing now remains from his time. His mansion, known to us from the representation on Phillip's map of 1685, appears to have been a fairly tall Elizabethan house set in the midst of spacious gardens within the area now enclosed by Fountain Street, Castle Place, and Corn Market. It was described by an early writer who saw it in 1635 as "a dainty, stately palace which is indeed the beauty and glory of the town", but it only lasted a century before it was accidentally destroyed by fire in 1708. It was abandoned and never rebuilt. The last remnants of its masonry were finally cleared from the site early this century, the gardens having long before been built over.

Belfast remained little more than a provincial market town for quite a long time and was languishing in obscurity when the Fifth Earl of Donegall succeeded to the trusteeship in 1757. From that time on the fortunes and shape of Belfast were to change. Favourable leases were granted to the inhabitants which were to lead to the physical improvement of the town. The Earl himself erected such buildings as the Old Exchange and Assembly Rooms and the Parish Church of St Anne at his sole expense, and also granted sites to the townspeople for such buildings as the Poor House and the Brown and White Linen Halls. Of these, only the Poor House (now called Clifton House) still stands intact as the earliest surviving building in Belfast.

It is appropriate in a way that the Poor House should be the first building to be discussed in the illustrated entries which follow in this book because the building of it was an event of major importance for the future of the town. In the organisation and funding of it the citizens of Belfast demonstrated their independence of their landlord for the first time. It was that spirit of independence, newly revealed, and the growing self-confidence of the townspeople during the following half-century that really made the town a success.

From the 1780s to the 1820s immense progress was made in terms of both commerce and intellectual development. The first effective steps were taken to improve the harbour; shipbuilding and iron founding were established; banks were formed; the chamber of commerce was set up; educational establishments and societies of an intellectual nature were founded; a library was formed and eventually a museum was opened. The public spirit displayed by the citizens in all this earned for the town the name of 'Athens of the north'.

Some of the built achievements of this time, including the broad streets that were laid out, still remain to this day, although the late Georgian stamp to the town has all but disappeared. The industrial expansion and commercial success through the remainder of the 19th century brought rapid changes to the size, fabric and character of Belfast. The great staple industry of linen manufacture made a tremendous impact. By the mid-Victorian years there were linen warehouses and offices in the neighbourhood of Donegall Square and Bedford Street, whilst factories and mills lay a bit further out. There were many streets of small terrace houses for the workers near the mills and there were large mansions in the suburbs for the merchants.

By the turn of the century Belfast, by this time a city by Royal Charter in 1888, was very prosperous. It was the chief seat and trading centre of linen manufacture in the world; in shipbuilding, marine engineering, and machine making it was in the front rank; and in rope making, distilling, and tobacco manufacturing it was well to the fore. It was by this time very well endowed with public buildings, churches, colleges, hospitals, and banks. A large number of these Victorian and Edwardian buildings have survived and it is their variegated and often colourful appearance that perhaps gives the city its most distinctive character today.

Following the heyday of the Edwardian era the fortunes of the city were more mixed. There was economic depression in the 1920s and 30s but this downturn was then replaced by a slow growth in prosperity. Building continued through these decades, some of it very fine and distinctive, but Belfast remained very much a Victorian and Edwardian city in physical character. There have been periods of destruction in the city – a considerable amount occurred at the time of the 2nd World War and also from the 1960s onwards as a result of redevelopment and to a lesser extent as regards civil strife and bombings – but through it all a fine series of buildings has survived.

Scope

This is an illustrated guide to the historic architecture of the city of Belfast and its immediate environs.

The main body of the book is the series of illustrated entries on buildings of architectural interest in the urban area of the city, dating from the late 18th to the mid 20th century. The coverage is very comprehensive up to the end of the 1930s with all the main buildings and many of the minor buildings given an individual illustrated entry. In addition to this, other buildings are briefly mentioned in some supplementary notes.

There is also a small selection of entries for the 1940s, 50s and 60s highlighting buildings which I feel to be of particular significance. There is merit in including these recent buildings in a historical guide, as they have qualities which arouse curiosity as to who designed them and when they were built. The story of style would be incomplete without them. The numerous more recent building projects are too new to have a place in what is essentially a historical survey of our architectural heritage.

Layout

The entries are set out in two sections, one dealing with the city itself, the other with the environs.

The extent of the city and environs has not been determined by strict adherence to municipal boundaries but rather by historic and architectural expedience. Such important buildings as Knockbreda Parish Church and Parliament Buildings, which appear now to be well within the city spread, are nevertheless kept out of the city sequence and are dealt with in the environs. When originally built they were clearly outside the city. At the same time the likes of Cregagh Estate which was built outside the municipal boundary at the time can nevertheless be included within the city sequence here without distorting the chronology.

The extent of the environs stops short of such built-up areas as Holywood to the northeast and Dunmurry to the southwest, yet strikes out as many miles distant to the south along the Lagan Valley. This is an area of tourist and recreational attraction not too far from the city and it is felt that the churches and other interesting buildings there should be identified. Belfast itself is a relatively modern settlement with no buildings of real antiquity and so the visitor might well appreciate being directed a fairly short distance out of the city to the nearest example of such a nationally important building type as the Irish Round Tower.

The area covered to the north stops short of Greenisland and Carrickfergus but is extensive enough to include the nearest example to Belfast of a 17th century fortified Plantation house, and also the finest

Celtic Revival church in Ireland, two important regional or national building types not covered within the sequence of city buildings.

The arrangement of the guide is chronological rather than topographical except that the environs are treated as three separate areas – north, south and east – although the arrangement is still chronological within those sections.

In general the entries appear in a fairly strict chronological order but occasionally the precision of the sequence is broken to allow a number of buildings by the same architect to be grouped together.

Numbering of entries

The city entries are numbered from 1 to 237 consecutively.

The environs are split into three areas with the buildings numbered consecutively within those areas and given the relevant prefix – N for northern, S for southern and E for eastern area.

These numbers appear at the relevant positions on the map guides.

Format of the entries

A pattern is followed whereby the name and address of the building is given along with the name of the architect, the date, and the name of the builder if known. In the description which then follows there is reference to such matters as the style, materials, original function, and any special points of interest about the building, as well as the names of craftsmen and artists who may have contributed to the furnishing or decoration. This description is usually brief but is extended for some important buildings.

In naming or titling the buildings the general approach has been to refer to a building by its most long-standing or traditional name. In some cases this has taken precedence, with the prefix *former*, over the latest owner's or tenant's name board or sign.

As regards the dates given for the buildings, an explanation is needed. When more than one date is given the first may be taken as the date the drawings were prepared or the date the foundation stone was laid (depending on the information available), whilst the later date is that of completion, or, in some cases, the official opening. When only one date is given it is usually, but not invariably, that of the design rather than that of the completion of construction.

Supplementing many of the 264 main entries are brief references to other buildings by the same architects or brief notes on neighbouring buildings, but only where they are not the subject of separate illustrated entries themselves. Information is thereby given on more than 200 additional buildings and monuments of interest in the city and its immediate environs.

Using the book

The chronological approach that has been adopted gives a clear visual picture of how architecture developed here through two centuries. The work of a particular period can be seen by turning immediately to the illustrated entries where dates are given.

Any specific building or area can be checked by reference to the numbered map guide (for those buildings that have illustrated entries) or by reference to the 'Buildings and Streets' index which lists both main entries and those extra buildings which are mentioned in the supplementary notes. This index can be used as a topographical guide by referring to the names of streets and localities which are given some prominence in it.

The output of individual architects, engineers, artists and craftsmen can be found through their relevant indexes.

Author's Acknowledgements

The author gratefully acknowledges assistance from the following: the staff of Belfast Central Library, Art Reference Section; John Gray of the Linen Hall Library; Karen Latimer, Architecture Librarian at Queen's University; Ivan Ewart of the Photographic Unit, Queen's University; Colin Hatrick of the Historic Buildings Branch, DOENI; Mr M.A. McFerran, Chief Building Control Officer, Belfast City Hall; Noel Nesbitt of the Ulster Museum; Robin Sweetnam, formerly of the Harbour Office; and the owners and custodians of a number of buildings illustrated and described.

Special thanks are due to Shaun Adair for printing the majority of the author's own photographs; to Dr Brian Walker and Mrs Margaret McNulty for reading the typescript and making many helpful suggestions; and finally to Miss Gillian McConnell for her careful typing of the manuscript.

Photographic Credits and Sources of Illustrations

The illustrations listed here are identified by their page number and their position on the page. The positions are noted in alphabetical order starting with the illustration furthest to the left and nearest the top of the page and working down each column.

All the photographs used were taken by the author except for the following: 21b, 41c, 69d, 101a, 109b, 109c, from the Welch Collection; 28a, 76c, 80b, 88a, 95c, 103a, 109a, 111c, from the Hogg Collection; and 13b, 22a, 27a; all courtesy of the Ulster Museum.

Illustrations taken from printed sources are as follows: 3b, 104b from G. Benn, *History of the Town of Belfast*, Belfast, 1823; 3c from J.R. Fisher and J.H. Robb, *Royal Belfast Academical Institution Centenary Volume 1810–1910*, Belfast, 1913; 9a from Mr and Mrs S.C. Hall, *Ireland: It's Scenery, Character etc.*, Vol III, London, 1843; 14c from R.M. Young ed., *The Town Book of the Corporation of Belfast 1613–1816*, Belfast, 1892; 14b from A. Stratton, *Elements of Form and Design in Classic Architecture*, London 1925; 13a, 67b from R.M. Young, *Belfast and the Province of Ulster in the 20th Century*, 1909; 16a from *Views in Belfast and the North of Ireland*, Marcus Ward, Belfast, nd [*c.*1860]; 21c from J. Dewar, *A History of Elmwood Church*, Belfast, 1900; 22b, 49b from *The Industries of Ireland*, Belfast, 1891 (reprinted by Friar's Bush Press, Belfast, 1986); 25b, 27c from D. Dunlop, *Life of W.J. Barre*, Belfast, 1868; 35a from *The Book of the Fete*, Queen's College, Belfast, 1907; 38a, 42c from L. Ewart, *Handbook of The United Diocese of Down, Connor and Dromore*, Belfast, 1886; 55c from D.J. Owen, *A Short History of the Port of Belfast*, Belfast, 1917; 60c, 61a from *A Monograph of the City Hall*, Belfast, 1906; 67a from *Academy Architecture* (1), London 1900; 95a from *An Exhibition of Architecture: Souvenir Handbook*, R.S.U.A., Belfast, 1951. 34b is taken from *The Dublin Builder*, 1864; 38b, 39b, 45b, 45c, 57a, 58c, 60a, 71a, 71b, 72c from the same journal, renamed *The Irish Builder and Engineer*.

Illustration XIIb is reproduced courtesy of P. and B. Rowan; 35b is by courtesy the Linen Hall Library; 36a by courtesy S. McKinney; and 60b by courtesy the Town Clerk; Plate XII by courtesy of the Grand Opera House; Plate XVIII is by kind permission of the Clerk to the Northern Ireland Assembly; Plate XIX by courtesy of the Supreme Court Administrator.

Sources of Information

The prime source of information was the files of drawings and registers of building applications dating back to 1861 which are held in the Building Control Office in Belfast City Hall. I am particularly grateful to the Chief Building Control Officer for having granted me access to this very useful collection.

The other most important source of information was *The Dublin Builder*, begun in 1859 and renamed *The Irish Builder* in 1868. This journal regularly reported on the state of the building trade in Belfast and frequently provided illustrations and descriptive accounts of Belfast buildings. It is available on microfilm in the Public Record Office of Northern Ireland and in The Linen Hall Library.

A large number of other printed sources were used for information on specific buildings. They ranged from *The Builder*, *The Architect and Building News*, and *The Dictionary of Architecture*, three English architectural periodicals of the nineteenth century, to the many locally published centenary and souvenir books on individual churches, public buildings, schools, convents, and banking companies. Some nineteenth century historians' works were also useful, in particular those of G. Benn, J.H. Smith, J.A. Pilson, W. McComb, and J. O'Laverty.

The most useful recent publications were C.E.B. Brett's *Buildings of Belfast*, London, 1967 (reprinted by Friar's Bush Press, Belfast, 1985), and Brian M. Walker and Hugh Dixon's *No Mean City*, 1983, and *In Belfast Town*, 1984, both published by Friar's Bush Press.

x

MAPS
This page: the city and surrounding area. Facing page: enlargement of central area.
Numbers relate to illustrated entries.
Based upon the Ordnance Survey maps with the sanction of the Controller of HM Stationery Office. Crown copyright reserved.

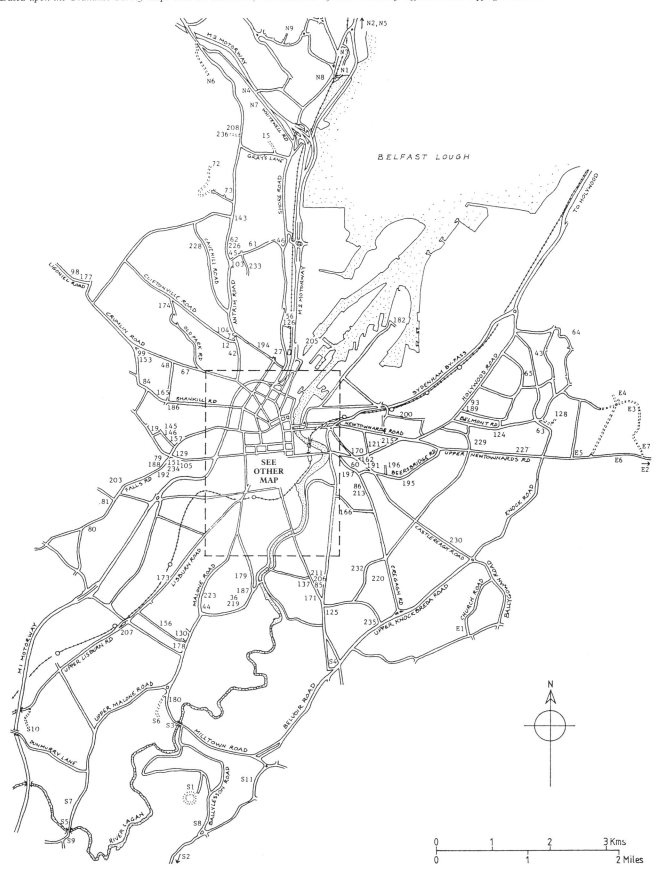

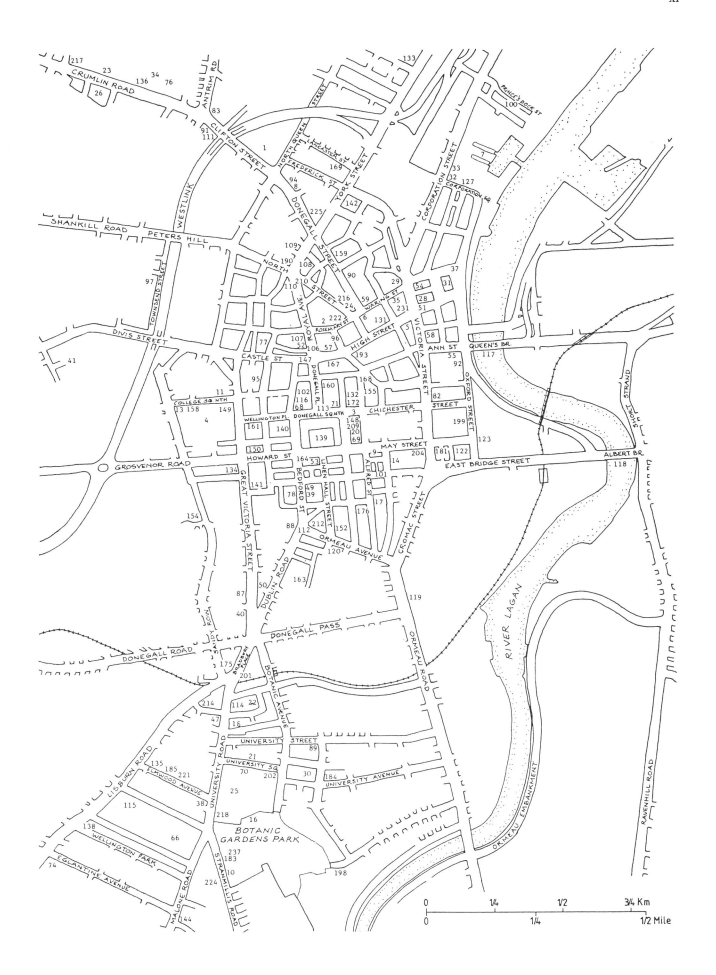

Clifton House: main front

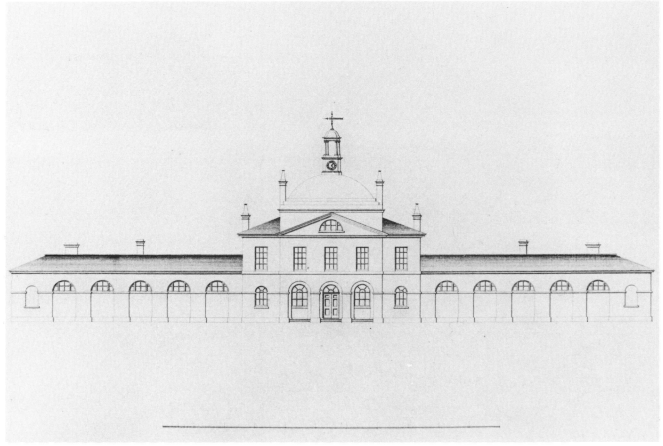

Clifton House: Robert Mylne's original proposal

Part One

THE CITY

Arranged chronologically

1 **CLIFTON HOUSE** (originally the Poor House), North Queen Street.
Robert Joy, 1771–4.

The Charitable Society's Poor House and Infirmary which opened in 1774 is the oldest complete surviving building in Belfast. Built with funds raised by public subscription and a lottery, on ground given by Lord Donegall, it provided accommodation for aged and infirm poor and an assembly room for the use of the townspeople. The earliest properly recorded medical service in Belfast was also connected with it. In two centuries its function has hardly changed: today it serves as a residential home and hospital for the elderly.

It is a rather strange sight with its tall octagonal stone tower and spire rising from the middle of a five-part pedimented brick composition laid out like a Neo-Palladian country house: an odd combination certainly but nevertheless a very charming piece of Irish Georgian building. The master masons were Joseph McNary and William Anderson, and James Brown who erected the spire. The master carpenter was Hugh Dunlop.

For a long time the Poor House was credited to the Dublin based architect Thomas Cooley who was indeed consulted by the building committee, but it was actually built from plans produced by an amateur, Robert Joy, a local paper merchant. Joy's design was clearly based on a set of drawings prepared by the eminent London architect Robert Mylne. In 1770 Mylne had been paid 40 guineas for a design which showed a large dome and lantern over the central block of a partly colonnaded development around four sides of a courtyard. Some features of this design were taken over by Joy although it was to take a century before the courtyard was completely enclosed. The end blocks of Joy's front were extended back in 1821 and 1825 on the south and north respectively. These two returns were further extended in 1871–2 to form the Benn Wings designed by William Hastings. The west side of the court between them is filled by the Charters Wing designed by William Barre in 1867.

Interiors of interest are the pleasant entrance hallway, the stairway with large Venetian window, and the first floor board room. In the corridors off the hallway can still be seen the walled-up Tuscan columns of the original open colonnaded walk (a feature taken by Joy from Mylne's scheme).

The laundry building standing detached to the north was designed in 1908, and the lodge at the main gate in 1938, both by Godfrey Ferguson.

A short distance to the north-west, in Henry Place, is the high-walled Clifton Street Graveyard, laid out in connection with the Charitable Institution. Established in 1797 on land given by the Earl of Donegall it was later enlarged in 1819. It has lain in a very bad state for some years with many of its monuments vandalised but repair work has now begun. Amongst the most impressive monuments is the Luke Memorial, a neo-classical sandstone mausoleum surmounted by an obelisk, by W. Graham *c.*1810.
See pl. I.

Clifton House: first floor landing

Clifton House: entrance hall

First Presbyterian Church: interior

2 FIRST PRESBYTERIAN (NON-SUBSCRIBING) CHURCH, Rosemary Street.
Roger Mulholland, 1781–3.

"The completest place of worship I have ever seen" wrote John Wesley in 1789 of this distinguished church whose plan was a perfect ellipse. The oldest surviving place of worship in the city, it was designed by Roger Mulholland, the first native architect to practise on any sort of scale in Belfast, with advice on the matter of pew arrangment from Francis Hiorne of Warwick. It had originally a two-storey classical frontispiece, its rusticated ground floor carrying Ionic pilasters with a pediment above. In 1833 the facade was brought forward and refaced in stucco with paired pilasters and a balustraded parapet. The pediments over the windows were also removed.

The interior is delightful, with box pews, a curving and swaying balcony on Composite columns, and a panelled plastered ceiling carried on plaster vaults. In 1906–7 the perfect ellipse was broken by Young and Mackenzie when the wall behind the pulpit was pushed out to accommodate a new organ.

There is a fine Neo-classical memorial to William Tennent who died in 1832, by Patrick MacDowell, and in the porch is a First World War Memorial with a figure of a heroic youth, by Rosamond Praeger, 1922. *See* pl. II.

3 7 – 11 CHICHESTER STREET. 1804.

Surviving members of what was originally a larger terrace built in brick in the standard Dublin style of the period. Nos 7 & 9 are of four storeys on a basement with steps up to Doric columned doorways in sandstone. No. 11 has been altered and now has a good Neo-Georgian shopfront, inserted by R. McKinstry in 1979.

The oldest surviving Georgian terrace in Belfast still stands at the top of Donegall Street, where nos 207–215 were built in 1791 and nos 201–205 followed in 1799, but it is badly in need of restoration.

7–11 Chichester Street

4 ROYAL BELFAST ACADEMICAL INSTITUTION, College Square East.
John Soane of London, 1809–14.

First projected in 1807, the Institution was intended as a grand educational centre combining the functions of a school and a university college. The eminent Neo-classicist John (later Sir John) Soane prepared his drawings free of charge as he said he wished to see such a noble project succeed. It started with extremely grand Greek Doric designs which proved too expensive to build and ended with very much less ambitious designs for a plain brown brick building with just a little architectural dignity given by a few strips of stucco. The semi-circular headed window above the Tuscan porch was originally left as a blank niche. The full effect of the main facade, closing the vista along Wellington Place and setting the tone for the later Georgian development of College Square, was spoilt when the large Technical Institute was built on the north lawn almost a century later.

New south wing, by R. H. Gibson, 1926; extended westwards in 1932 to absorb Watt, Tulloch and Fitzsimons's new classrooms of 1914. Single storey three-bay Dining Hall detached to the south, by Samuel Stevenson and Sons, 1955–7.

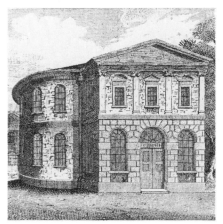

First Presbyterian Church facade

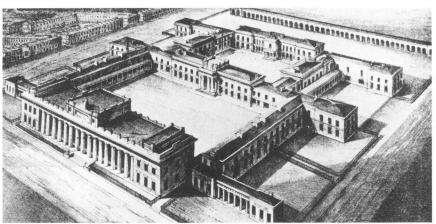

Royal Belfast Academical Institution: Soane's original proposal

Original front of church

Royal Belfast Academical Institution: main front

5 ST GEORGE'S CHURCH (Church of Ireland), High Street.
John Bowden of Dublin, 1811–12, incorporating a portico of 1788.

John Bowden fitted a fairly plain Georgian preaching box behind a splendid portico brought from the Earl Bishop of Derry's unfinished Ballyscullion House near Castledawson in Co. Londonderry which had been designed by either Francis Sandys or Michael Shanahan of Cork. The splendid portico consists of four giant Roman Corinthian columns carrying a steep pediment with attached columns and pilasters in a curved plane behind. The arms added to the pediment are of the see of Down and the town of Belfast. Inside Bowden's church is a gallery carried on 'Tower of the Winds' columns. Later additions to the interior are an elaborate open timber truss roof and a pulpit, both designed by W. J. Barre, 1867; new chancel by Edward Braddell, 1882; chancel screen designed by Braddell in 1885 but not built until 1928; and murals in chancel painted by Alexander Gibbs. The school to the rear was by W. Butler, 1885.

St George's Church

The Commercial Buildings

6 THE COMMERCIAL BUILDINGS (now Northern Whig printing works), Waring Street.
John McCutcheon, 1819–20.

An important landmark in the history of not only the architectural but also the commercial development of the town. The first really monumental public building in Belfast, it took over the function of the old Exchange which stood opposite it. It is not clear if McCutcheon actually designed this building or was merely employed to supervise the construction: he was referred to at the time as the "contracting architect". At any rate, the Commercial Building is a fine set piece in Dublin granite with small Doric porches and a big Ionic order carried over a rusticated ground floor. The carved panels display a version of the Belfast arms flanked by swags and trophies. Built by public subscription "for the benefit of the trade and the accommodation of merchants" it contained a Commercial Hotel in the east block, shops and offices in the west block, and a commer-

PLATE I. *Clifton House. The board room. See 1.*

PLATE II. *First Presbyterian Church, Rosemary Street. Interior. See 2.*

PLATE III. *Graymount. The hallway.* See 15.

PLATE IV. *St Malachy's Roman Catholic Church. Interior. See 17.*

PLATE V, *Sinclair Seamen's Presbyterian Church. Interior. See 32.*

cial news room in the centre with an assembly room above it. These interiors have been drastically altered over the years (by Robert Watt in 1886 and T. W. Henry in 1919), but still to be seen are the cast-iron Tuscan columns (one marked 'Belfast Foundery 1819') of the original colonnaded walk around an open court to the rear, now however mostly walled up and also roofed over.

7 CLARENDON DOCK BUILDINGS, off Corporation Square.
David Logan, 1825–6 (Henry, Mullins and McMahon of Dublin, builders).

The first dry dock here, Clarendon No.1 Graving Dock, was built from 1796 to 1800 by William Ritchie, the pioneer of shipbuilding in Belfast; the second dry dock, No.2, to the north, was completed in 1826 along with the dock buildings designed by the Scottish engineer David Logan. He was resident engineer at Donaghadee harbour at the time of his appointment by the Ballast Board in Belfast in 1823. The buildings comprise a long eight-bay sandstone arcaded workshop in the centre with a single storey engine house in basalt built across the east end, and a handsome two-storey stuccoed dwelling house for the Dock Master at the west end. Detached to the west stands a plain stone building which contained the furnace house for the tar boiler. The arcaded central building housed a carpenters' workshop, stores and sheds, on the ground floor, with rigging lofts above; the majority of its arches appear to have been originally open and then later filled in with windows in arched brick surrounds. The engine house may also have undergone some later work. Formerly a tall chimney rose from behind it. These dock buildings are now closed but together with their associated dry docks (and the Clarendon wet dock which was completed in 1851) they constitute a very important survival from the early days of the port of Belfast.

Clarendon Dock Buildings viewed across No. 1 Dock

8 ST PATRICK'S SCHOOL, Donegall Street.
1828.

The earliest surviving example of Gothic Revivalism in Belfast. Two red brick blocks linked by a gabled porch. A variety of window types is used, from small-paned Tudoresque with horizontal drip moulds to others more pointed in form, but all are regularly arranged across the facades. No architect's name is recorded but the form of openings, the handling of details, and the elaborate perpendicular tracery at this particular date all suggests Thomas Duff of Newry.

Became a National School in 1832 (the first in Belfast to do so); later run by the Christian Brothers; now closed.

St Patrick's School, Donegall Street

May Street Presbyterian Church

9 PRESBYTERIAN CHURCH, May Street.
William Smith, 1828–9 (John Brown, builder).

A fine classical church of red brick with stucco dressings. The Neo-Palladian front has a portico *in antis*, and columns and pilasters in Roman Ionic style with well modelled capitals of the angular type established by Scamozzi. Fine interior with gallery curved around three sides on Ionic cast-iron columns. The later coffered timber ceiling; the pulpit; and the Cooke Memorial doorway, a Roman triumphal arch, were all by John Boyd, 1870. The portrait medallion was executed by John Foley RA, of Dublin.

Alongside the church is the school with a small Roman Doric order on very high pedestals and curious fluted Ionic keystones to windows; by John Boyd, 1858–9 (L. & T. Browne, builders).

10 GATELODGE TO FRIAR'S BUSH GRAVEYARD, Stranmillis Road.
1829.

A plain Gothick symmetrical cottage with pointed arch and windows and spikey finials to buttress piers. The architect or builder is not recorded but possibly the same hand can be seen shortly afterwards at old St Mary's Roman Catholic Church, Shore Road, Greencastle, 1831.

Friar's Bush graveyard was the chief burying ground for Catholics until Milltown opened in 1869. Among the more interesting monuments architecturally are two High

Gatelodge to Friar's Bush Graveyard

Victorian Gothic examples, the Read Memorial wall slab probably dating from the 1870s, and the McKenna Memorial of 1872, a canopy with spire.

11 **OLD MUSEUM**, College Square North.
Duff and Jackson, 1830–1.

The first museum in Ireland to be erected by voluntary subscriptions, built by the Belfast Natural History and Philosophical Society. The Society was started in 1821 by eight enterprising young men who had in view the formation of collections of specimens. Within ten years they were able to open this building, and for almost eighty years it flourished and did duty in Belfast as a public museum. Generally accepted as the work of the young Thomas Jackson, it is a scholarly piece of Greek Revivalism with details compiled from various Athenian sources. The sloping architraves to some windows echo those of the Erechtheum; the laurel wreaths across the frieze number eleven, like those of the Choragic Monument of Thrasyllus; and the very distinctive water leaf and acanthus capitals of the portico are copied from those on the Tower of the Winds. The most notable interior feature is the ironwork gallery round four sides of the uppermost room with its gracefully curving stairway.

The fine pair of houses with Neo-Grec detailing adjoining on the right were built about the same time and were probably also by Jackson.

The Old Museum

12 **26–30 CLIFTONVILLE ROAD**
(Home for the Blind until recently).
Thomas Jackson, 1831–2.

The most impressive survival of a villa estate which Jackson laid out as a speculative venture in the 1830s, inspired by the Clifton area of Bristol where he had trained. Hence the name Cliftonville for this part of Belfast. In its original state it must surely have been one of the most important early suburban developments in Ireland. A Doric order, laurel wreaths and a band of anthemion ornament are amongst the Greek Revival motifs that decorate this very unified terrace of three houses. Note the giant scale of the mutuled eaves and also the windows that peer between the triglyphs of the frieze – an idiosyncratic touch to spice an otherwise heavy brand of Neo-classicism.

The other houses in the development have now gone except for the semi-detached pair at 34 & 36 Cliftonville Road. These are treated in a more abstract manner with plainer attic and no Doric order, but with good Regency ironwork porches.

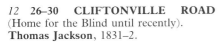

26–30 Cliftonville Road

26–30 Cliftonville Road: eaves detail

13 **CHRIST CHURCH** (Church of Ireland), College Square North.
William Farrell of Dublin, 1833.

A fine example of a late Georgian Neoclassical facade. Greek Revival in style with an Ionic *in antis* porch. Stone fronted but the rest of the church is in brick. Galleried interior much altered in 1878 with a new panelled ceiling and unusual pine pulpit, designed by William Batt.

Christ Church

14 **14–26 JOY STREET** and **39 & 41 HAMILTON STREET**.
Early 1830s.

A plain but handsome block of red brick terrace houses. It provides a good illustration of late Georgian housing for the merchant class. Nicely restored by the Northern Ireland Housing Executive from 1984–6.

15 **GRAYMOUNT** (latterly a school), Gray's Lane.
Thomas Jackson, *c*.1835.

A very fine Regency house built on a slope overlooking Belfast Lough for William Gray, a linen merchant. A typical Jackson house of the period, finished in stucco with coupled pilasters across the front and a central Ionic tetrastyle portico. Very fine Neo-classical detailing to interior with bold panelled ceilings and good marble fireplaces. An Ionic hall screen leads to an impressive double return stair with a big spacious lantern soaring above.
See p. III.

14–26 Joy Street and 39 & 41 Hamilton Street

Graymount: the lantern

Graymount

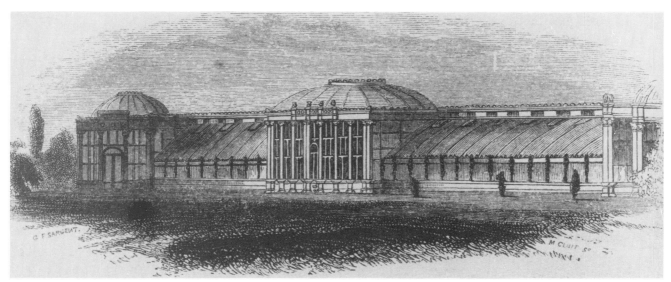

The Palm House: Lanyon's original proposal

The Palm House

16 THE PALM HOUSE, Botanic Gardens, Stranmillis Road.
Charles Lanyon

Wings, 1839–40 (constructed by Richard Turner of Dublin); central dome, 1852 (constructed by Young of Edinburgh).

One of the oldest surviving examples of a curvilinear iron and glass structure anywhere. Its two wings are in fact the earliest known work of the renowned ironmaster Richard Turner of the Hammersmith Works in Dublin, pre-dating by some years his Glasnevin Conservatory (1842–50) and his greatest achievement, the Great Palm House at Kew (1844–8). Lanyon's original design for the Palm House here, with a shallow domed rectangular centre block and domed square end blocks, gave way in the end to the present bulbous oblong dome placed between wings. After falling into a bad state of disrepair the Palm House was renovated, and re-opened in 1983.

The Botanic Garden was established here in 1829 by the Belfast Botanic and Horticultural Society. It became 'Royal' in 1840. The present layout is basically similar to that of the mid nineteenth century, although there have been many changes in detail.

South of the Palm House is the Tropical Ravine House, originally the seven-bay Fernery built in 1886 with a Dutch gable possibly by William Batt, extended westwards to more than double its length in 1900, and re-roofed in 1980. It is a possibly unique interior with a peripheral balcony walk around a man-made sunken glen.

At Stranmillis Road entrance to gardens, is a Statue of Lord Kelvin by Albert Bruce Joy of Dublin, on a pedestal designed by Richardson and Gill of London, 1912. The entrance gate piers were designed by W. Batt, 1875.

At the southernmost end of the grounds at Stranmillis Embankment opposite King's Bridge is the decorative domed cast-iron Jaffe Memorial Fountain, originally erected in Victoria Square, 1874.

St Malachy's Roman Catholic Church

17 ST MALACHY'S ROMAN CATHOLIC CHURCH, Alfred Street.
Thomas Jackson, 1840–4 (Ross & Campbell, builders of shell 1841–2; Peter Lundy, builder for interior 1842–4).

The result of a competition with fourteen entries. A striking sight, in red brick with stone dressed castellations and octangular corner turrets. One of the most original Tudor Revival churches in Ireland with a really splendid interior. The west porch front follows the usual English collegiate chapel models, but behind it Jackson eschews the ecclesiological layout. The church spreads out on a lateral plan with the altar placed on one of the longer walls to achieve the greatest amount of gallery accommodation around three sides. The whole flat ceiling of this transverse rectangular auditorium-like room is densely patterned with stuccoed conoidal pendant vaults and ribs in imitation of Henry VII's Chapel, Westminster Abbey.

The original altar, pulpit and sanctuary rails of unpolished Irish oak were all replaced by marble in the renovation of 1926 which also saw the sanctuary floor laid in mosaic and the east wall screened in perpendicular tracery. This looks like the work of

St Malachy's Church: interior

Padraic Gregory. High altar recently set back in a recess leaving the reredos paintings by Felix Piccione undisturbed. Lourdes Shrine installed in front porch, by P. Gregory, 1932. Central belfry tower on church added in 1868 but later rebuilt without spire.

Presbytery alongside church was by O'Neill and Byrne, 1869.
See p. IV.

18 2 & 4 MOUNT CHARLES
1842

A pair of neat little two storey stuccoed Regency Greek Revival villas. Bold corner pilasters, slim Doric columned porches, and sarcophagi-like chimney stacks replete with acroteria. Architect's name not recorded but most likely Thomas Jackson. Both houses damaged by a bomb in 1973; subsequently restored. No. 2 so badly damaged by another bomb in 1974 that almost total rebuilding was necessary; this was carried out by R. McKinstry and M. Brown in 1982. It is now the headquarters of the Royal Society of Ulster Architects.

2 Mount Charles

19 CLONARD HOUSE (now Convent of Sisters of Charity of St Vincent de Paul), Clonard Gardens.
Thomas Jackson, c.1843.

Originally set in parkland of trees and shrubs and green fields, but now surrounded by streets of houses. A fine stuccoed villa of Regency type, symmetrical with two-storey bows to each end. Essentially Neo-Classical with coupled pilasters across the front and a tetrastyle Ionic portico, but with a Georgian Gothic fanlight. Built for the Kennedys, flax spinners. Architect's name not recorded but must surely be Thomas Jackson. It is his style of house and he did build the Kennedy's weaving factory at Millvale, Falls Road, 1843–4 (now gone).

Clonard House

20 METHODIST CHURCH, Donegall Square East.
Isaac Farrell of Dublin, 1846–7 (James Carlisle, builder).

A very solid looking classical church with an imposing Roman temple front. It consists of a great hexastyle Corinthian portico with a rusticated arcade behind. The recessed porch is vaulted over which adds to the feeling of weightiness. Interior and roof rebuilt in 1850 after a fire the year before but the entrance front remained intact.

Next door to the right, the former garage and offices designed for Harry Ferguson by Tulloch and Fitzsimons in 1926.

Donegall Square Methodist Church

University Square

21 4–30 UNIVERSITY SQUARE
Attributed to **Thomas Jackson**, 1848–53.
Nos 1–3 by **Thomas Jackson and Son**,
1870.

One of the best formal terraces in Ulster.
Three-storeyed in brick with painted
dressings and recessed Doric porches, it is a
regular and unified composition apart from
some later bay windows and other minor
alterations. Some of the later doors and
fanlights of the early 1900s are quite attractive with their pretty leaded light patterns.
At No. 22 there is a nice little Edwardian
wrought iron grille.

It was probably inevitable that by the time
Nos 1 and 3 were added to the terrace they
would stand out from the earlier work. They
are taller and chunkier in a High Victorian
way, with a Gothic motif in the gable attic
window.

Upper Crescent

22 UPPER and LOWER CRESCENTS,
off University Road.
1846 and 1852 (James Corry, builder).

The concave Upper Crescent of 1846, with a
giant Corinthian order applied to the centre
and ends, all finished in stucco, is the grandest Neo-classical terrace in Ulster. The
straight-run Lower Crescent of 1852 is in the
same vein but its layout seems never to have
been fully completed. It has also suffered
more alterations than the earlier terrace.
The architect's name has not been recorded
for either of these but certain details such as
the pierced balustrades and the rich
Corinthian order suggest the hand of
Charles Lanyon.

At the west end of Lower Crescent is the
former Victoria College, by Young and
Mackenzie, 1873–4; the much altered block
at the east end was by William Hastings,
1876. The block at the west end of Upper
Crescent was also by Hastings, 1869.

Lower Crescent

23 THE PRISON, Crumlin Road.
Charles Lanyon, 1843–5, with additions
1849–50.

Italian Renaissance Mannerism came into its
own with Lanyon's County Gaol or 'New
House of Correction' as it was sometimes
called. Built of black basalt from quarries in
the nearby hills with Scotch sandstone
dressings. Laid out on the model of London's Pentonville with four long ranges radi-
ating from a central hall now mostly hidden
from view except the tall well modelled
ventilating shaft. Part of the entrance lodges
with their gates between can also still be
seen. Wholly rusticated including its screen
of Tuscan columns, this was a delightful
little block, solid and appropriate like a 16th
century fortified Italian city gate in the manner of Sanmicheli.

The Prison: a general view in the nineteenth century

The Prison: a nineteenth century view of the governor's house

14

Northern Bank, Waring Street, photographed in the inter-war era

Sir Robert Taylor's Assembly Room: now completely remodelled

24 NORTHERN BANK (formerly Belfast Bank), Waring Street. **Charles Lanyon**, 1845.

Clearly inspired by Charles Barry's London club houses of the 1830s Lanyon here uses the Italian Renaissance palazzo style. A big eaves cornice, aedicule window surrounds with pediments and attached columns, and bold quoins at the corners are just some of the characteristic features of this well massed block. This is in fact a remodelling in stucco of the old Exchange building already on the site. It had started in 1769 as a single storey arcaded market house which was converted to Assembly Rooms in 1776 with the addition of an upper storey, by the

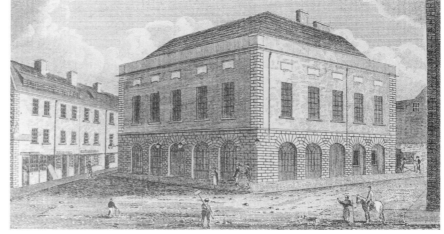

The Old Exchange and Assembly Rooms: now remodelled

prominent London architect Robert Taylor. Lanyon remodelled this five-bay building but allowed Taylor's splendid classical interior (as recorded in Thomas Malton's aquatint of 1792) to remain. That fine coffer-vaulted and pilastered treatment disappeared, however, in W. H. Lynn's remodelling of the interior in 1895. Thus whilst it can be claimed that this is the earliest public building still standing in Belfast, the Old

Exchange and Assembly Rooms as they were in 1776 have in fact now disappeared from view.

Extensions on North Street side by W. H. Lynn, 1875, and G. P. & R. H. Bell, 1956. Two storey link block with columned porch added to Donegall Street side, and roof and chimneys of Lanyon's block raised, with lantern added on top, by Tulloch and Fitzsimons, 1919.

25 QUEEN'S UNIVERSITY,
University Road.
Charles Lanyon, 1846–9 (Cranston Gregg, builder).

One of the three Queen's Colleges set up in Ireland in 1845 to provide non-denominational higher education (the others were at Cork and Galway). Not built exactly as Lanyon had first intended, many of his proposed ornamental details as well as other more important elements, being pruned by the Board of Works to keep cost within limits set by Parliament. Nevertheless Queen's is still substantial enough to rank as the highpoint of Early Victorian architectural achievement in Ulster.

A long two-storey composition punctuated by towers with no real attempt to be truly quadrangular, it was clearly designed for maximum pictorial effect on its open site. Built of glowing red brick with some dark blue brick diapering and with freestone dressings it is a spendid sight seen across its lawns through the screen of trees. Appropriately for a college it was designed in Tudor style, with a specific Oxonian model chosen for its central feature. The 15th century Founder's Tower at Magdalen College was here copied fairly closely but tidied up and made taller and narrower in proportion and thinner and crisper in detail. Detailing elsewhere in the building is fairly repetitive and uninspired, but the use of flying buttresses for balusters to porches on the south side is a novel and witty touch. Interiors of note are the large windowed entrance hall, and the Great Hall with carved angels on the hammer-beams.

The South Wing Extension with tall tower and arch was by W. H. Lynn, 1911–12 (H. Laverty & Sons, builders); the small block between it and Lanyon's building was inserted by W. A. Forsyth of London, 1933

Queen's University

(W. Dowling, builder). The North Wing Extension and tower were by John Mac-Geagh, 1951. The Music Department (originally Students Union) and the Old Library are described elsewhere. Main entrance gateway, designed 1943; new Physics Building to south, 1955–61; and Main Library tower block to north, 1967, were all by John MacGeagh. The War Memorial standing in front of the main building was designed by Sir Thomas Brock of London and executed by F. Arnold Wright, 1923.

Queen's University: Charles Lanyon's original proposal

The County Courthouse

St Paul's Church of Ireland

26 **COUNTY COURTHOUSE**,
Crumlin Road.
Charles Lanyon, 1848–50 (James Carlisle, builder).
Remodelled by Young and Mackenzie, 1905 (McLaughlin & Harvey, builders).

Clearly a really magnificent building in its original state. It was designed in a Neo-Palladian style with a deep hexastyle portico, flanked by well modelled wings with giant Corinthian pilasters and triple arched porches. The fine proportions and details of Lanyon's building were destroyed, however, when the building was enlarged in 1905. New end blocks were added, recessions filled in, and the whole was encased in stucco. Interior also altered, but at least Lanyon's portico still remains, surmounted by a figure of Justice by Joseph Kirk, RHA, of Dublin. The Court House is connected to the prison on the other side of Crumlin Road by means of a subterraneous passage.

27 **ST PAUL'S CHURCH OF IRELAND**, York Street.
Charles Lanyon, 1850–1.

A pleasant little Early Victorian sandstone church in Early English style, with its chancel next to the road. The general handling and range of carefully studied detail suggests the hand of William Henry Lynn, Lanyon's chief assistant at the time. North aisle added later, 1872, probably by Welland and Gillespie of Dublin. The metal tie bars fixed to each roof truss of nave were added after war damage in the air-raids of 1941.

28 **TRUSTEE SAVINGS BANK**
(formerly Northern Bank Head Office), Victoria Street.
Charles Lanyon, 1851–2.

A vigorous piece of Neo-classicism with Neo-Palladian touches which shows Lanyon's regard for Sir Robert Taylor: the front facade is a more mannered and elaborate version of Taylor's original design for Salisbury Guildhall. The well modelled surfaces with vermiculated rustications, the arches set within arches, and the play of larger and smaller orders are all indicative of Lanyon's lively and robust manner. The gigantic window surrounds to normal sized windows together with the big Roman Doric columns combine to create an impressive effect in a building only one principal storey in height. Of Portland stone on a grey granite plinth.

Trustee Savings Bank, Victoria Street

29 Former **CORN EXCHANGE**,
Victoria Street.
Thomas Jackson, 1851.

A fairly plain two-storey building with shops below a lofty first floor hall, erected by a company of the grain merchants of Belfast. Built of freestone, rusticated and pilastered, with a very tall Renaissance loopwork parapet, and an Ionic *in antis* porchway.

Former Corn Exchange

30 **UNION THEOLOGICAL COLLEGE** (originally the Presbyterian College), Botanic Avenue.
Charles Lanyon, 1852–3 (John Corry, builder).

Built of freestone from Scrabo quarries, the design was placed first in a field of twenty entries in a competition for which no premiums were offered. A powerful Renaissance Revival set-piece, somewhat mannered with shades of Adam and Vanburgh as well as various Italian masters. Ground floor rustication is a little bit fussy, but the general massing is simple and good, and the giant Roman Doric columns and high consoled attic make for a magnificent centre piece. The deep recessed and vaulted porch leads to a twin-columned hallway with double-return staircase. Very fine library interior on first floor with Corinthian columned screens.

South wing by Young and Mackenzie, 1868–9; north wing and chapel by John Lanyon, 1878.

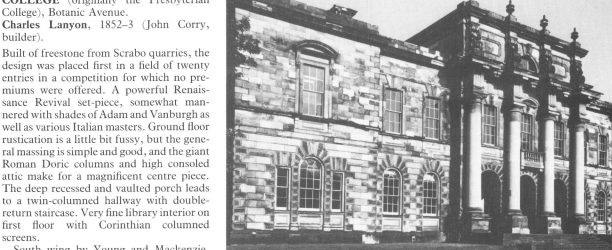

Union Theological College

The Custom House: detail of river front   *The Custom House*

31 **THE CUSTOM HOUSE**, Custom House Square.
Lanyon and Lynn, 1854–7 (D. & J. Fulton, builders).

The Italian Renaissance palazzo style is here majestically used on a Palladian plan, with the building arranged round three sides of a raised open court approached by a flight of steps. Entirely built of Glasgow freestone. Heavily rusticated and arched main storey, with Corinthian aedicules to the floor above. This is continuous around the building except for the more elaborate central entrance bays of the courtyard and river fronts (the original recessed porch to the latter is now built up). Fine carved angels in the river front spandrels, representing Manufacture, Peace, Commerce and Industry. These were designed by Samuel Ferris Lynn the sculptor brother of the architect William Henry Lynn, but were executed by Thomas Fitzpatrick who also carved the figure group in the pediment showing Britannia flanked by Neptune and Mercury.

32 **SINCLAIR SEAMEN'S PRESBYTERIAN CHURCH**, Corporation Square.
Lanyon and Lynn, 1856–7.

A Lombardo-Venetian corner composition in Scrabo stone showing Lynn's interest in the writings of Ruskin. An L-shaped church with a bold campanile alongside joined only by an arcaded flying staircase link to the gallery. Boundary railings added 1865.

The church was built to serve visiting seamen. With the arrival of Rev. Samuel Cochrane in 1902 the interior took on a very pronounced nautical flavour, with the addition of a pulpit desk shaped like the prow of a ship; sets of port and starboard lights on the organ, desk and pulpit; a binnacle installed as a font in 1927; collection boxes in the shape of lifeboats; a clock like a ship's wheel, and memorial plaques in anchor, sail, and bell shapes, erected in the 1920s. The inner porches with Arts and Crafts style leaded lights were added in 1927.   *See* pl. V.

Sinclair Seamen's Presbyterian Church

33 Former **SAILOR'S HOME**,
Corporation Street.
Lanyon and Lynn, 1857–8.

A rather severe looking Gothic Revival
building in Scrabo sandstone, clearly the
work of W. H. Lynn. Mostly Early English
style with typically long and narrow lancets
and a sprinkling of quatrefoils across the
facade, but a touch of Decorated Gothic
style is introduced in the delicate curvilinear
line of the small windows to the dormers.
Well modelled chimneys with big weathered
caps relieved by little gablets; these are
characteristic of the firm's early Gothic
style, as are the mask or notch-head label-
stops to the porch.

34 ST PAUL'S CONVENT OF
MERCY, Crumlin Road.
J. J. McCarthy of Dublin, 1855–7; wings
and cloisters 1859 (Thomas Byrne, builder).

The only work in Belfast by 'The Irish
Pugin' as the great Gothic Revivalist James
J. McCarthy was known. More colourful
than usual for McCarthy's work, being built
in red brick with blue brick relieving arches
and Scottish sandstone details. Decorated
Gothic in style with some fine traceried windows. Built around four sides of a central
garden.

Additional storey to the north wing, 1925,
and south wing, 1937, added by Frank
McArdle.

The chapel added by T. J. O'Neill, 1909,
next to the road, was demolished recently to
make way for an extension to the Mater
Hospital.

Former Sailor's Home

St Paul's Convent of Mercy: interior of corridor

St Paul's Convent of Mercy

Ulster Bank, Waring Street

35 ULSTER BANK, Waring Street.
James Hamilton of Glasgow, 1857–60
(D. & J. Fulton, builders).

Belfast's finest commercial building, an exuberant and ornate Renaissance palazzo, the magnificent result of a competition which attracted 67 entries. Shades of Palladio and ancient Rome combined, in the arcaded front and two-storeyed portico of coupled Doric columns below with Corinthian above, surmounted by a very elaborate entablature. Built of Giffnock stone it is loaded with rich acanthus ornament, bearded mask keystones, numerous putti, and a fine emblematic figure group of Britannia, Justice and Commerce all carved by Thomas Fitzpatrick. The highly ornamental cast-iron balustrade and lamp standards were made by Laidlaw of Glasgow. Spacious columned banking hall lit by an octagonal stained glass dome. The four Aberdeen granite Corinthian columns display Science, Poetry, Sculpture and Music on their friezes. This and the rest of the elaborate stucco work was executed by George Crowe. The dome was decorated by Sibthorpe of Dublin with heathen deities and allegorical figures surmounted by portraits of famous people, but these have now been removed.

Ulster Bank, Waring Street: interior detail

Adjoining the bank to the right, are the Ulster Buildings by Thomas Jackson & Sons, 1869–70, in white Scrabo sandstone with Dungannon dressings and Newry granite plinth (John Murphy, builder); extended along Skipper Street by Blackwood and Jury, 1929.
See pl. VIII.

PLATE VI. *St Peter's Cathedral. Interior. See 41.*

PLATE VII.   *Allied Irish Bank, Royal Avenue. Interior. See 52.*

PLATE VIII. *Ulster Bank, Waring Street. Interior. See 35.*

PLATE IX. *St Mark's Church of Ireland, Holywood Road. Interior. See 93.*

PLATE X. *Gas Works Offices. The stair hall.* See *119.*

36 STRANMILLIS HOUSE, Stranmillis College, Stranmillis Road.
Lanyon, Lynn and Lanyon, 1857–8.

Multi-gabled Jacobean style house built for Thomas G. Batt, a director of the Belfast Bank. Originally it had an open belfry and ogee pyramidal roof to the corner tower but these have been removed. The original entrance porch and a low wing to the north were replaced by a large extension in simplified Elizabethan style in 1924 after the house became a college, probably to the design of Roland Ingleby Smith, chief architect to the Ministry of Finance.

37 CALDER MEMORIAL FOUNTAIN, Albert Square.
George Smith, 1859.

A little Italian Mannerist essay in sandstone, with voluted pilasters like upturned consoles. Designed by the Engineer to the Harbour Commissioners to contain "a drinking fountain for the use of bipeds and a trough for the use of quadrupeds", as the *Dublin Builder* put it. Erected to the memory of Commander Calder RN, founder of the Belfast Society for the Prevention of Cruelty to Animals.

Stranmillis House before the alterations of 1924

Calder Memorial Fountain

38 ELMWOOD HALL (formerly Elmwood Presbyterian Church), University Road.
John Corry, 1859–62 (Henry Martin, builder).

Lombardo-Venetian in style, with a lofty storeyed tower and spire and an arcaded loggia across the front, designed by a talented amateur John Corry. He had earlier been the builder for Lanyon's Presbyterian College but here, inspired no doubt by the writings of John Ruskin, he displayed an unusually exotic artistic ability in this fine High Victorian church. The architectural treatment is very rich, with arcading, coupled windows, carved freizes, and corbel courses. The capitals of the loggia present a fine series of plant studies, each one different, probably carved by the Fitzpatricks.

Former Elmwood Presbyterian Church

These are very much in Ruskinian taste as are the 'eyes of coloured marble' above them. Scrabo sandstone of pinkish hue was used to face the church, but a yellower sandstone was employed for the tower and spire. It was not actually erected until 1872 (Robert Corry, builder). There is a wide and spacious interior with good plasterwork but the fine pulpit and other furnishings have been removed, and the stained glass windows have been replaced by pseudo-Georgian glazing bars. Former school rooms and lecture hall to rear of church added 1866; former manse to south side in 1872; and boundary rails, gates and piers in 1873, all to the designs of John Corry.

Ulster Hall: Barre's original proposal for interior

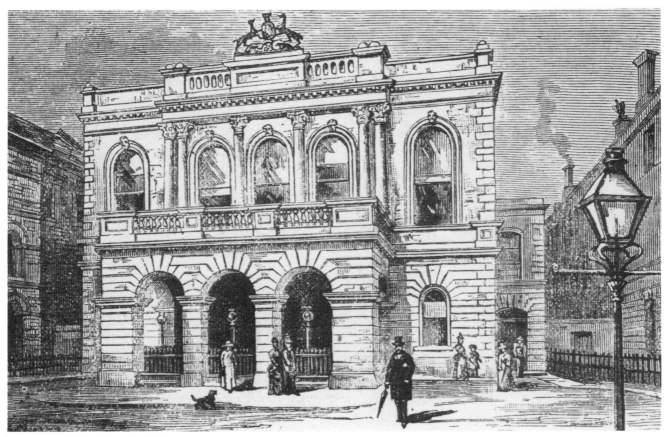

Ulster Hall: exterior sketched c.1891

39 **ULSTER HALL**, Bedford Street.
William J. Barre, 1859–62 (D. & J. Fulton, builders).

One of the largest music halls in the British Isles when first opened, the result of a competition won by a young architect from Newry, Co. Down. Italianate in style with rustications, hairy mask keystones and Roman Corinthian columns, finished in painted stucco. Originally an open portico or *porte-cochere* stood at the front for carriages, but that was later closed up, and a cast-iron verandah added by W. H. Lynn, 1882. Additional blocks to each side of the *porte-cochere* were added by R. B. Donald, City Surveyor, *c.*1933.

The interior of the hall is impressive although never as splendid as Barre intended. Galleried, with arcaded walls, it houses a really magnificent organ presented by the wealthy industrialist Andrew Mulholland in 1862.

Great Victoria Street Presbyterian Church

40 **GREAT VICTORIA STREET PRESBYTERIAN CHURCH**,
Great Victoria Street.
1860–1.

Known as Sandy Row Presbyterian Church when first opened this is a boldly detailed and solemn piece of classicism, with giant engaged square columns laid over a rusticated front. Rather over-scaled freize and blocking course. Possibly designed by John Boyd who in partnership with William Batt added a school house to the rear in Albion Street in 1868.

41 **ST PETER'S CATHEDRAL** (Roman Catholic), St Peter's Square.
Jeremiah McAuley, 1860–6 (John Ross, builder for the main body of the church; Murphy & Connor for the interior).

Designed by an architect turned priest, Father Jeremiah McAuley who had trained with Thomas Jackson before being ordained in 1858, this impressive Gothic Revival church is a prominent landmark in the Falls Road area. Continental cathedralesque in form with twin western spires and a big traceried window in the gable above a good typanum sculpture of the Liberation of St Peter. Built of Scrabo sandstone with Scottish stone dressings. The spires were added by Mortimer Thompson in 1886 (Henry Fulton, builder). The interior is notable for its tall hammer-beam roof but some effect has been lost in the recent rearrangement of the sanctuary and crossing area. Original north and south porches enlarged to make side chapels by Padraic Gregory in 1946. He also designed a new high altar and a very fine marble baldachino.

Presbytery to rear designed by John O'Neill, 1867. He succeeded McAuley as supervising architect for the cathedral in 1862.
See pl. VI.

St Peter's Cathedral

42 **DUNCAIRN PRESBYTERIAN CHURCH**, Antrim Road.
William J. Barre, 1860–2 (John Lowry, builder).

In 14th century Gothic style in Scrabo stone with a tower and spire beside the main gable, Barre's original church was T-shaped, but over the years it has grown in size. First the south aisle and conical stair tower were added in 1871; then the north aisle in 1884; and finally the organ chamber in 1906, all by Young and Mackenzie. Galleried interior with a good hammer-beam roof. The first Presbyterian church in Belfast to have a bell hung in a tower.

The school house which Barre designed as part of the group was replaced by Young and Mackenzie's Sinclair Hall in 1914–15 but the original manse still stands behind the church. It is a fine and characteristic piece of Barre's domestic work entirely in sandstone with chunky chamfered chimneys, half-hipped gables and a single buttress to the front porch. Enlarged to the rear by Young and Mackenzie, 1875.

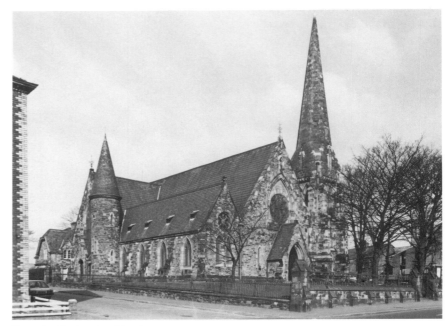

Duncairn Presbyterian Church

43 **THE MOAT**, Motelands, Old Holywood Road.
William J. Barre, 1863–4.

Barre's most colourful house, in glowing red brick with sandstone dressings and blue stone bands. Built for Thomas Valentine, a linen merchant. Bold shapes and vigorous detail especially to the chimneys and a very fine series of large sandstone capitals to the entrance loggia. The sculptor's name is not recorded but such a wealth of Ruskinian naturalism with birds, nests, snakes and botanical specimens could only have been worked, in Belfast, by the Fitzpatricks.

The Moat

44 **DANESFORT** (now Headquarters of Northern Ireland Electricity), Malone Road.
William J. Barre, 1864.

One of the finest High Victorian mansions in Ireland, Danesfort (originally known as Clanwilliam House) was built for the linen magnate Samuel Barbour. It is a more majestic although less colourful version of The Moat. Italian arcades, Tudor chimneys and a French chateau tower-roof are just some of the wide range of elements brought together in this highly sculpturesque composition. Good bold vegetal carving to the *porte-cochere* capitals and fine pierced stone balustrading to the balconettes. Some splendour inside too with large rooms grouped informally around a central hall and staircase.

The Gothic Revival gate-lodge to the Malone Road is clearly later and is not by Barre. It looks like work of the late 1870s. Architect not known.

Danesfort

45 FORTWILLIAM PARK UPPER GATEWAY, Antrim Road.
William J. Barre, 1864.

At the upper end of this residential park, stand these four large Gothic Revival piers of sandstone, still with traceried wing walls but without their original decorative iron gates. The little towered gate-lodge alongside was also designed by Barre.

46 FORTWILLIAM PARK LOWER GATEWAY, Shore Road.
Architect and date not known.
Probably built *c.*1870.

At the lower end of Fortwilliam Park stands a pair of classical archways, but now without their decorative iron gates and the lodge that once stood alongside. It is certainly not by Barre as has often been supposed. Two possible architects who come to mind are the Glaswegian James Hamilton who is known to have built a large mansion in the park (that was Dunlambert, 1871–3, now gone), and local man Thomas Turner who used banded masonry on occasion. The central pier which used to stand between the arches here is now to be found just inside the gateway of Musgrave Park, Stockman's Lane.

Fortwilliam Park Upper Gateway when first complete

Fortwilliam Park Lower Gateway

47 METHODIST CHURCH,
University Road.
William J. Barre, 1864–5.

A good corner composition, Lombardo-Romanesque in style, and boldly detailed in polychrome brick and sandstone. Dominated by the handsome square tower, flat-planed and crisp-edged in a way that would have pleased Ruskin. The centre window on front facade is a new arrangement replacing a small plate-traceried rose window damaged by a bomb in 1973. Fine interior, entirely unspoilt.

School to rear along Fountainville Street, beyond the side turret, added by J. A. Moncrieff, 1869.

University Road Methodist Church

48 Former **EDENDERRY MILL** (now Industrial Estate), Crumlin Road. **William J. Barre**, 1865.

This long five-storey red brick block was the largest linen mill in Ulster at the time it was built. Among various additions over the years are the blind arcaded brick boundary wall by James Ewart, 1869; the new engine house built onto the south side of the mill, by Browne Brothers, 1908; and the gate-lodge by Edwin Kennedy, 1914, now badly spoilt.

On the opposite side of Crumlin Road is the former Ewart's Mill designed by James Ewart, 1865; extended eastwards along Crumlin Road by S. Stott of Oldham, 1903. In the next block west is the former Brookfield Mill established 1850 and enlarged in the 1860s and 70s.

Former Edenderry Mill

49 **BRYSON HOUSE**, Bedford Street. **William J. Barre**, 1865–7 (James Henry, builder).

A very fine and vigorously detailed High Victorian linen warehouse in medieval Italian palazzo style. Typical Barre touches are the short stumpy columns over the doorways and the big stone capped chamfered chimney-stacks corbelled out in brick.

50 Former **OPHTHALMIC HOSPITAL**, Great Victoria Street. **William J. Barre**, 1867 (R. & H. Fulton, builders).

An attractive round-arched polychrome facade in white brick with bands of red. The sandstone strings and dressings have now been painted over. Extended by one bay to the south in matching style by Blackwood and Jury in 1928.

Bryson House

Former Ophthalmic Hospital

51 **ALBERT MEMORIAL**, Queen's Square. **William J. Barre**, 1865–9 (Fitzpatrick Brothers, builders).

The competition for the design of a memorial to the Prince Consort was won by Barre in 1865. It is a High Victorian version of the 'Big Ben' Clock Tower at Westminster, but in place of Pugin's late English Gothic detail we have here Barre's favoured eclectic mix of styles including Early French and Italian Gothic, with early Renaissance heraldic lions to the flying buttresses at the base. Unfortunately the tower was built on sleechy slobland at the head of an old tidal dock, with the town river coursing around its foundation, and this led to its present rakish angle. This development combined with some defects in the masonry led to the removal of much of the ornamental carved work on and around the octagonal belfry stage in 1924. As a result the tower now looks rather bare at the top. Also removed was the elaborate stone canopy over the statue of the Prince but the full-length figure, shown in the Robes of a Knight of the Garter, still remains; it was sculpted by S. F. Lynn. The clock, of a construction similar to that of Westminster tower, was made by Francis Moore of High Street.

The Albert Memorial: Barre's original perspective drawing

stone carver named Barnes of whom nothing else is recorded in Belfast. The exterior is now rather more polychromatic than was ever intended by Barre; it has been painted from as early as the 1880s to arrest the decay of its white Cookstown sandstone. It is also less elaborate than he had first hoped. On grounds of expense he was forced to omit a grand figure group in high relief intended to fill the pediment and a further group intended for its apex.

Inside, the banking hall is truly magnificent, with its square central area lit by a tall circular dome over an octagonal arcade carried on stumpy corbelled columns with big Early French Gothic capitals. The gnomish stucco figures in the groin angles are supposed to represent Mechanism, Engineering, Art, War, Law, Navigation, Architecture and Industry. After Barre died in 1867 the work was supervised by Turner and Williamson.

See pl. VII.

Allied Irish Bank, Royal Avenue: Barre's drawing of banking hall

Allied Irish Bank, Royal Avenue

52 ALLIED IRISH BANK (formerly Provincial Bank), Royal Avenue. **William J. Barre**, 1864–9 (R. & H. Fulton, builders).

A very richly ornamented building both inside and out, typically High Victorian in its handling of diverse styles from Romanesque to Neo-Palladian. Massive arcaded front with clustered columns and Early French capitals, and heads of Irish soldiers and ancient provincial kings, carried out by a

Allied Irish Bank, Royal Avenue: one of the modelled figures inside

Yorkshire House in 1911

53 YORKSHIRE HOUSE, Donegall Square South.
1862–3.

Built as Jaffe Brothers' linen warehouse, this is a building very much changed for the worse over the years – its stone walls painted over, its windows altered, and its once prominent street-front chimneys removed – but it is still worth observing for the series of sculpted heads in the roundels. These represent various mythical, cultural, inventive and other historic figures, and are all clearly named. No architect's name has been recorded but the original chimneys, some window details, and the mouldings to arches suggest Thomas Jackson. Nor is a sculptor's name recorded but Thomas Fitzpatrick seems most likely; he did very similar heads on the Theatre Royal, Arthur Square in 1871 (demolished).

Alterations, including false ceiling and arches in porch, for the Yorkshire Insurance Company, were by R. H. Gibson, 1929. Part of the premises along Linen Hall Street were replaced by a tower block for the same company, by Gibson and Taylor, 1956.

54 HEYN OFFICES, 10 Victoria Street.
Thomas Jackson and Son, 1863 (John Lowry & Son, builders).

Built for the Scottish Amicable Life Assurance Company this was the first purpose-designed insurance office block in Belfast. A massive and ornate building in what was known at the time as the 'modern Italian'

Heyn Offices

style, it has some of the air of a Venetian Renaissance palazzo. Its crowded and busy facades were carried out in Dungannon sandstone and white Glasgow brick, whilst the entire building was designed to be fireproof with stone staircases used throughout – a sensible example for an insurance company to set.

55 RIDDEL'S WAREHOUSE

(now closed), Ann Street.

Thomas Jackson and Son, 1865–7 (William Nimick of Holywood, builder).

Designed no doubt by the son, Anthony Jackson, this four-storey warehouse was built for one of the leading metal merchants in Ireland. A typical High Victorian mixture of round and segmental arcaded storeys, in polychrome brick and stone: Newry granite to the ground floor and white Glasgow brick above, with dressings of Dungannon sandstone and Armagh and Whitehaven limestone. Before it was blocked up some years ago the central archway led to a courtyard covered with an iron and glass roof and surrounded by five galleries running round the entire rear of the building.

Next door on the corner with Oxford Street is the later Bank of Ireland, by Miller and Symes of Dublin, 1899.

56 Former JENNYMOUNT MILL OFFICE BLOCK, North Derby Street. 1864.

The earlier range of mill buildings here, dating from 1856, are very plain but this addition of 1864 has an interesting series of carved keystone heads of famous literary and other figures. The inscriptions are not very legible but an attempt can be made to identify the people represented. They appear to be as follows. Ground floor, left to right: Wordsworth, Burke, Peel, Galilei, Columbus. First floor, left to right: Johnson, Goldsmith, Newton, Scott, Shakespeare, Burns. Those on the end elevation are unidentified.

No sculptor's name is recorded but it might well have been the Fitzpatrick Brothers. Nor is an architect's name recorded but John Lanyon's later involvement elsewhere on the site leads one to suspect the presence of Lanyon, Lynn and Lanyon here.

Riddel's Warehouse

17 Castle Place

Former Jennymount Mill office block

57 17 CASTLE PLACE.

William Hastings, 1864 (Fitzpatrick Brothers, builders).

A typical High Victorian facade of mixed materials and architectural styles, orginally built as Thompson's Restaurant. Carved owls and bats appear amongst the fruit and other ornamentation. Ground floor altered in 1917 by W. Eccles of Liverpool who also balustraded the first floor windows.

Hastings also designed the big five-storey block for John Robb & Co. nearby on the corner with Lombard Street, 1876.

McCausland's Warehouse: carved representations of the five continents. Left to right: Africa; Asia, Oceania, Europe, America

58 LYTLE'S AND McCAUSLAND'S WAREHOUSES (now closed), Victoria Street.
William Hastings, 1866-7 (Fitzpatrick Brothers, builders).

A pair of adjoining seed warehouses built for rival firms in what was termed at the time as the "modern Classic style freely treated". Both are palazzo-like with ornamental four storeyed facades of nearly equal frontage, with uniform storey heights marked by strings, cornices, and parapets; but the character of each is different. McCausland's, to the right, is in a form of Italianate classical style, but Lytle's is more Romanesque in style. The decorative treatment differs too with a mainly vegetal and animal nature to the carving of Lytle's whereas a continental theme is apparent next door. On Lytle's we find owls and eagles, chicks in nests, nibbling squirrels, and rows of tortoise heads peeping out of the carved stone foliage. The harp and crown on the parapet was the firm's trademark. There is good High Victorian wrought iron work too, showing John Lytle's monogram. The five massive piers of McCausland's are carved with representations of the five continents and their botanical and commercial products. From left to right they are *Africa*, an Ethiopian with a lily of the Nile and a broken chain, and bananas, gourds and date palms; *Asia*, a Chinese girl draped in silk with peacock feathers and palms, pomegranates, rice and tea plant; *Oceania*, a South Sea islander with cocoa-nut palms, bread fruit, yams and other Polynesian products; *Europe*, a male head with conventional ornament "denoting the superiority of art in this continent", with vines, pineapples, melons, figs, flax, grain and fruit and foliage; and *America*, a feather-head-dressed Indian with tomahawk and arrows, and tobacco, cotton and Indian corn. These were all designed by Michael Fitzpatrick, a junior partner in the firm which built and sculpted both warehouses.

Lytle's and McCausland's Warehouses

Lytle's Warehouse: detail of carving

59 **3 DONEGALL STREET**.
William Hastings, 1867.

A High Victorian facade with a rather mannered treatment to some elements, such as upturned consoles, over-large capitals on too thin colonettes, and tapering flat pilasters: inelegant, to say the least.

Next door on the corner with Waring Street is a much more ordinary block by Thomas Jackson and Son, 1871.

3 Donegall Street

60 **MOUNTPOTTINGER PRESBYTERIAN CHURCH**,
Castlereagh Street.
William Hastings, 1868–9.

Good strong detailing characterises this High Victorian round-arched church. In particular note the robust finial, the conventionalised foliage of Early French type, and the very stylised stiff-leaf work. Stair turrets flanking the front were by William Gilliland, 1886. School and hall to rear were by Thomas Roe, 1892.

As well as church and commercial work Hastings was also responsible for a few hospitals. The only one still standing, although closed, is The Samaritan, Lisburn Road, designed in 1874.

Walton

61 **WALTON** (Dominican Convent), 38 Fortwilliam Park.
*c.*1865.

A two-storey Italianate sandstone house, originally with another storey to its tower. One of the few surviving mansions built in this private park in the 1860s and 70s, this is probably the house known originally as Morven, erected for the linen merchant Henry Kirk. No architect is recorded but some details suggest the Glaswegian James Hamilton. A similar hand can be detected at the lower gateway to Fortwilliam Park.

School block to the north, 1950, and chapel to the south, 1960s, both by Kilpatrick and Bready. Beyond the school block is Fairbourne by Vincent Craig, 1908, an Edwardian manorial style house, now part of the school.

62 **BARNAGEEHA**, in the grounds of St. Patrick's School, Antrim Road.
Probably late 1860s.

A sandstone villa in the manner of Alexander 'Greek' Thomson of Glasgow. Now hemmed in by modern school buildings and very much altered, with modern fenestration to the upper floor, the original staircase replaced, and the topmost stage of the lantern removed. Nevertheless, the arrangement of the bays, the form of the original chimneys and lantern, and the idiosyncratic use of Greek detail are all characteristic of that celebrated Scot's remarkable style, although it appears that this house was not designed by him. He had a number of close followers in Scotland and the design was probably the work of one of them.

Mountpottinger Presbyterian Church

Barnageeha

Ormiston House

63 **ORMISTON HOUSE**, Hawthornden Road.
David Bryce of Edinburgh, 1865–7.

A thoroughly Scottish House, Baronial in style, designed by the leading Scots architect of the time, and built for James Combe who had come from near Edinburgh to settle in Ulster. Crowstepped gables and a bartizan turret are picturesquely combined with other elements of Scottish 16th century architecture. Plenty of surface detail, with stringcourses, gargoyles, and improving inscriptions such as "He That Tholes Overcomes". An architect's panel appears on the side of the entrance tower.

64 **GLENMACHAN TOWER**, Glenmachan Road.
Thomas Jackson, 1860s.

This towered Italianate house, built for Sir Thomas McClure, is the most splendid of a series built in the area to the designs of Thomas Jackson. Others on Glenmachan Road are the towered Lismachan, 1870; the more modest Glen Ebor (now Hampton), *c.*1863; and Altona, 1864, Jackson's own residence. The fine Glenmachan House, Holywood Road, of early 1860s, initially built for Jackson himself, but then sold to Sir William Ewart, was demolished in recent years.

65 **CRAIGAVON** (now a hospital), Circular Road.
Thomas Jackson, 1870.

This Victorian villa in Italianate style set in extensive grounds was built for James Craig, a highly successful businessman who became a millionaire. One of his sons, Vincent, became an architect in Belfast; another, James, later Lord Craigavon, was to become the first Prime Minister of Northern Ireland and later owned the house himself. The glazed loggia and Neo-Palladian billiard room to the right appear to have been later additions, probably of the 1880s, and look like the work of W. H. Lynn.

66 **METHODIST COLLEGE**, Malone Road.
William Fogerty of Limerick, 1865–8 (James Henry, builder).

William Fogerty won the limited competition for the Wesleyan Methodist College with a Gothic Revivalist design, mainly fourteenth century English in detail. It presents a bold and effective group of buildings in red Belfast brick with dressings of freestone from Glasgow, all on a base of Scrabo sandstone. Built in stages: the central portion and east wing were built first; the west wing followed in 1871. Good iron lamp standards at main entrance. Sanatorium added at the rear by John Boyd in 1874.

In 1879 a porter's lodge was built at the Lisburn Road end of College Gardens by John Lanyon. It is a picturesque little Gothic Revival building with a fish-scale slated conical-roofed stair turret. The 'W. M. C.' in a quatrefoil stands for Wesleyan Methodist College.

Glenmachan Tower

Craigavon

Methodist College

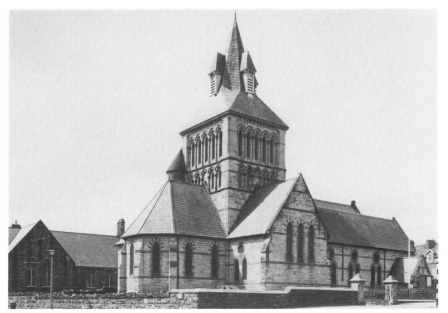

St Mary's Church of Ireland

The Linen Hall Library

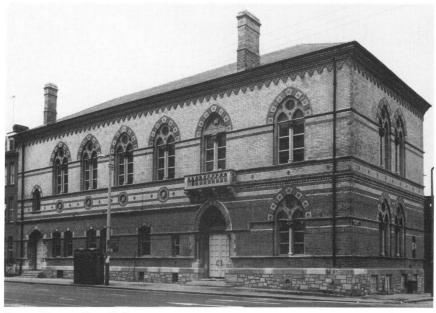

Former Clarence Place Hall

67 ST MARY'S CHURCH OF IRELAND, Crumlin Road.
William Slater of London, 1865–8 (James Henry, builder).

A nicely sited High Victorian church in Gothic style, mainly of white Scrabo stone with bands of red, although Scottish stone was used for the massive square tower at the crossing. Arcaded, with broached slated roof and tall hipped lucarnes this tower gives the church a very continental look. The original intention was for William Slater, a leading London architect, to build this as a model church particularly in the matter of economy in which local architects were supposed to have had much to learn. The original cost was to have been £2,400; in the event it exceeded £6,000! Roof and interior ruined in the war time blitz of 1941; replaced by Dennis O'D. Hanna with steel trusses over nave, 1945.

Behind the church is St Mary's Schools: the eastern part built first, by W. H. Lynn, 1882; the rest added by S. P. Close in similar style, 1903.

68 THE LINEN HALL LIBRARY, Donegall Square North.
Lanyon, Lynn and Lanyon, 1864.

Originally Moore and Weinberg's linen warehouse, it became the Linen Hall Library in 1892. Built of Scottish fire brick with Scrabo stone dressings it has a modest exterior with no notable features except the festoons of linen carved around the doorway. The chief interest is in the institution itself. It began in 1788 as the Belfast Reading Society, changing its name to the Belfast Society for Promoting Knowledge in 1792. Another change of name followed when from 1801 the library was accommodated in the White Linen Hall in the centre of Donegall Square. It moved here when that site was purchased by the City Council in 1890 and the City Hall eventually built there. The conversion of the warehouse to a library was carried out by Young and Mackenzie in 1891.

Next door, to the right, is the former Belfast Bank (now shops and offices) in Dumfries red sandstone by W. H. Lynn, 1895.

69 Former CLARENCE PLACE HALL, May Street.
Lanyon, Lynn and Lanyon, 1865–6 (Fitzpatrick Brothers, builders).

Originally a hall, reading rooms and offices for the Church of Ireland Young Men's Society, this is the most colourful of W. H. Lynn's Italian Gothic works. In red, white and blue banded and diapered brickwork, with sandstone plate tracery, foliated capitals, and ornamental balcony, it was more likely inspired by George Edmund Street's *Brick and Marble Architecture in Italy* than by Ruskin's *Stones of Venice*

70 **OLD LIBRARY, Queen's University**, University Road.
Lanyon, Lynn and Lanyon, 1865–8 (James Henry, builder); extended by W. H. Lynn, 1911–14 (H. Laverty & Sons, builders).

Originally built at the height of the eccle-siform Gothic fashion and then extended in similar style, the old library looks at first glance like a college chapel, its parts laid out like a nave and chancel with transepts, in rather Italian polychrome brick with plate traceried rose windows and grotesque Early French gargoyles. Built in two distinct phases: the original building was the chimneyed hall with five cross gables on a squarish plan designed in 1865; all the rest to the west, including the elaborate ventilator turret, followed nearly half a century later. It was in 1910–11 that W. H. Lynn won the competition for various extensions to the University. Part of this entailed enlarging his own earlier library building which he did in very fine style. What was once a really magnificent High Victorian Gothic interior however has been badly spoilt by recent insertions. Worth noting inside on a wall of the former porch near the south west corner is a commemorative plaque with relief portrait of Lynn. North porch and four low windows in the western gable were added by John MacGeagh, 1951.

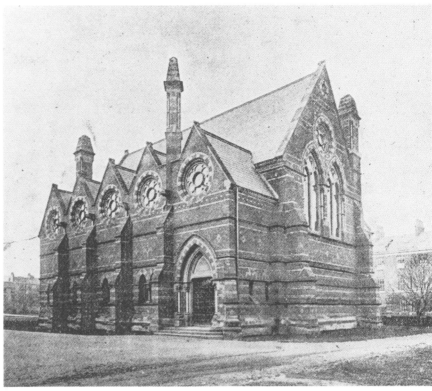

Old Library, Queen's University, before the extension of 1911

71 **Former RICHARDSON SONS AND OWDEN'S WAREHOUSE** (later the Water Office; now part of Marks and Spencer), Donegall Square North.
Lanyon, Lynn and Lanyon, 1867–9 (James Henry, builder).

A colossal pile of red sandstone designed by W. H. Lynn, "an eclectic of the eclectics" as he was known to his contemporaries. It is a fine essay in Florentine Gothic with a strong Venetian feel to the circles introduced in the spandrels. The window rhythms are also Venetian with those in the middle run together in continuous arcades; in the milder climate of Venice they could have been open loggias. Very French corbelled tourelle to one side and, before war damage in 1941, there were steep French roofs with Neo-Gothic dormers and massive chimney stacks. On the corners, a nice illustration of Ruskinian naturalism where the carved foliage of the colonette capitals creeps onto the wall. The rampant lion in the ground floor roundels is the crest of the Richardson family and the original firm's trademark. No harm was done by the recent remodelling of the building inside as the original High Victorian interiors were destroyed in the 1941 blitz.

Former Richardson Sons and Owden's Warehouse, photographed before 1886

Belfast Castle: perspective sketch by J.J. Phillips

72 **BELFAST CASTLE**, Downview Park West, Antrim Road.
Lanyon, Lynn and Lanyon, 1868–70 (W. B. McMaster, builder).

Standing on the southern slope of Cave Hill commanding a magnificent view of the lough and the city, Belfast Castle is a large mansion in Scottish Baronial style which harmonises well with the rugged character of the mountain scenery behind. It was built for the Marquis of Donegall apparently to designs of John Lanyon, prepared around 1865. Stone from the demesne was used for general building with a facing of Cookstown sandstone and dressings of white Scottish stone. A picturesque pile of gables and turrets outside, but the interior generally lacks drama. Rather baroque exterior stairway added to garden front in 1894; architect's name not recorded but may have been John Lanyon.

Castle and grounds presented by the Earl of Shaftesbury as a gift to the city, 1937.

Now cut off from the castle by inter-war housing, the former **Gate Lodge** looks a curious sight in Antrim Road at Strathmore Park, with its small turreted jumble of stepped gables and chimneys; by John Lanyon, *c*.1870.

Belfast Castle: the garden staircase

Belfast Castle: stairway

Belfast Castle: entrance portico

Former Belfast Castle gatelodge

73 Former **BELFAST CASTLE CHAPEL** (later known as the Chapel of the Resurrection), Innisfayle Park. **Lanyon, Lynn and Lanyon**, 1865–9 (John Lowry, builder).

Almost certainly the work of Lynn rather than the Lanyons. In Decorated Gothic style, four bays in length with an apsidal end and octagonal turret, but very craggy with many rough-hewn uncarved blocks. Originally built as a mortuary chapel by the third Marquis of Donegall as a memorial to his son the Earl of Belfast who died in 1853. Transferred without endowment to the Church of Ireland in 1938, it has stood empty in recent years, deconsecrated and vandalised. Patrick McDowell's white marble monument of the young Earl mourned by his mother, which the chapel was built to enshrine, has been moved to Belfast City Hall. Various wooden furnishings, carved saints and angels have also been moved, to St. Peter's Church, Antrim Road.

Belfast Castle Chapel

74 ST THOMAS'S CHURCH OF IRELAND, Eglantine Avenue.

Lanyon, Lynn and Lanyon, 1869–70 (John Lowry and Son, builders).

A very impressive High Victorian Gothic church, strong and bold in form, designed by John Lanyon. Built of white Scrabo sandstone banded with red, with red marble colonettes to the belfry and marble disks set in the stone spire. A typical piece of eclectic design, drawing on a variety of sources: Early French Gothic for the big nave capitals, Italian Gothic for the polychrome effects, and possibly also Early Christian Irish for the round stone-capped stair turret to the tower. Majestic interior with a good pulpit of Bath stone with Derbyshire spar crystals. Church extended to the south in 1888. A good group is formed with the rectory alongside, also polychromatic but in this case of red brick with blue and yellow brick stripes. Details to note on the rectory are the prominent well formed chimneys with battered brick caps, and the nicely carved sandstone angel playing a lute above the front door.

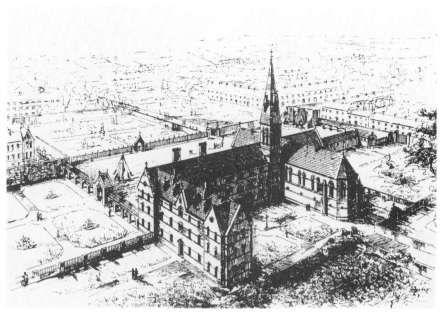

St Malachy's College: bird's-eye view sketched in 1869

St Thomas's Church of Ireland: sketch by J.J. Phillips

75 ST JAMES'S CHURCH OF IRELAND, Antrim Road.

Lanyon, Lynn and Lanyon, 1869–71.

Only the buttressed tower and spire remain of W. H. Lynn's Decorated Gothic building of 1869, the rest being destroyed in the blitz of 1941. The rebuilding by R. M. Close with freestone walls and Westmorland slates was also in Decorated style but not to the original design; it dates from 1946, and still looks new today.

Lynn's Gothic schools of 1872 alongside were extended and slightly altered by E. P. Lamont in 1957.

The former parsonage next door to the west on Cliftonville Road was designed by Thomas Drew, 1875.

76 ST MALACHY'S COLLEGE, Antrim Road.

John O'Neill, 1866–8 (Messrs. Byrne, builders).

This High Victorian rebuilding of the original Diocesan Seminary of Down and Connor, which had been established here at Vicinage House in 1833, consisted of a Christian Brothers Monastery block facing Crumlin Road and a classroom wing facing Antrim Road. A chapel wing and a belfry spire were not carried out as O'Neill intended. Additions by Mortimer Thompson, 1881–2, comprised the chapel to the north, a wing to the south, and the entrance gateway on Antrim Road. South wing extended by McLean and Forte in 1949 in matching style.

77 ST MARY'S ROMAN CATHOLIC CHURCH, Chapel Lane.

John O,Neill, 1868 (John O'Connor & Sons, builders).

The mother church of Roman Catholicism in Belfast, but nothing of the old chapel of 1783–4 is now visible. O'Neill's new work was in polychrome brick in Romanesque style, but behind its front facade of 1868 his church in turn was virtually rebuilt by Padraic Gregory with new apse, confessionals and sacristy, in 1940. Originally O'Neill's tower to the south side of the main front was carried up as a tall belfry, but has been truncated. The Lourdes Grotto and campanile in the garden were by P. and B. Gregory, 1953–4.

St James's Church of Ireland

St Mary's Roman Catholic Church

78 Former **EWART'S WAREHOUSE**, Bedford Street.
James Hamilton of Glasgow, 1869 (McCreary and Morgan, builders).

An extremely rich linen warehouse built of Scottish sandstone. Designed in the Venetian Renaissance style which James Hamilton had previously used to great effect in Glasgow when working there as an assistant to Alexander Kirkland in the 1850s. Originally erected for the Bedford Street Weaving Company it was later taken over by Ewart's. The extension along Franklin Street was by James Ewart, 1883; and to the rear, by Stevenson and Sons, 1937.

St Mary's Dominican Convent

Former Ewart's Warehouse

79 ST MARY'S DOMINICAN CONVENT, Falls Road.
John O'Neill, 1868–70.

A big gabled block by John O'Neill in round-arch polychrome brick with bold carved capitals; a beautiful piece of work in what might be called a 'Belfast Byzantine' style. Collegiate wing to the west in similar style was by O'Shea and E. and J. Byrne, joint architects, 1897. O'Neill's block was extended to the north east in perfectly matching style by Padraic Gregory, 1926. For his fine chapel in Gothic style of 1926 see separate entry. In the corridor of the convent, the stained glass window of Our Lady of Mercy with Dominican Saints was by Evie Hone, 1948.

Nearby to the south on Falls Road is St Mary's Training College by E. and J. Byrne, 1898, with chapel of 1902.
See also pl. XVII.

80 MILLTOWN CEMETERY GATEWAY, Falls Road.
Timothy Hevey, 1869–70 (J. & J. Guiler, builders).

A High Victorian Romanesque arched gateway, boldly detailed throughout, with chunky chamfered timber gates and big Early French capitals to the sweep wall piers, and very stylised iron boundary railings. Highly coloured with a variety of stones employed, namely white Scrabo sandstone for the general walling with bands of red Dumfries, Dungannon sandstone dressings, and Tullamore limestone colonette shafts. The tympanum over the arch was left rough but was originally intended to contain a carving of The Resurrection.

Hevey also designed the large Celtic cross of 1871 dedicated to the Reverends Clarke and Canavan, which stands centrally just beyond the gateway. It is covered with biblical scenes and panels of Celtic interlace. Clarke's was the first grave opened in this cemetery, in November 1869. Beyond it is a striking white limestone pinnacled and traceried Gothic vault to Matthew Bowen, 1876; architect not recorded but possibly Hevey. The much less elaborate Gothic vault to John Cramsie to the west was by Alex McAlister, 1879.

Milltown Cemetery Gateway: perspective sketch by the architect in 1870

81 **BELFAST CEMETERY**, Falls Road.
Laid out by **William Gay** of Bradford,
1866–9.

The cemetery was laid out to the plans of
Gay but the superintendant's house looks
like the work of John Lanyon of the mid
1870s. Vaults in Gothic style with good High
Victorian wrought iron railings also date
from the 1870s. Fountains in cast iron were
made by George Smith's Sun Foundry,
Glasgow.

Among the more interesting monuments
are the Herdman Memorial, a rare piece of
Egyptian Revivalism in Belfast, dating from
the 1870s; the Carson Memorial, an art
nouveau slab, a rarity in Ireland, dating
from 1905; the Pirrie Memorial of post-1924
with a bronze bust by London sculptor
Bertram Pergram and a plaque showing a
view of the Royal Victoria Hospital which
Pirrie was instrumental in building; and the
early 20th century Inglis Memorial slab with
fine relief panels undoubtedly by the
sculptress Rosamond Praeger of Holywood,
Co. Down. Prominent local architects are
commemorated in the very refined Lynn
Memorial slab *c*.1876 by W. H. Lynn who
died in 1915, and the more eye-catching
Late Gothic style Phillips Memorial Cross
c.1882 by J. J. Phillips.

Belfast Cemetery: Herdman Memorial

Belfast Cemetery: Carson Memorial

Belfast Cemetery: Inglis Memorial

82 Former **TOWN HALL**,
Victoria Street.
Anthony Jackson, 1869–71 (James Henry,
builder).

Two storeys of round-headed windows of a
sort of pseudo-Gothic type in red brick with
Dumfries red sandstone dressings, with
canopied doorways and a mansard roof: a
kind of Franco-Italian job but rather dull.
Besides the council chamber and corporation offices in the Victoria Street front the
original scheme comprised also various
courts, a police station, and fire brigade
station along Chichester Street.

The Fire Brigade Headquarters was not
built until 1892 and in a different form, to
the design of J. C. Bretland; enlarged 1900.
The Central Police Station was not built
until *c*.1897-1901 but has now gone.

On the other side of Victoria Street, on the
narrow angle with Upper Church Lane is the
former Trueman's Warehouse, by T. Jackson and Son, 1868.

Belfast Cemetery: The Phillips Memorial Cross

Former Town Hall

83 **ST ENOCH'S PRESBYTERIAN CHURCH**, Carlisle Circus.
Anthony Jackson, 1870–2 (James Henry, builder).

A jagged and craggy Gothic Revivalist pile in white Scrabo sandstone, now much blackened, originally with a tall crocketed stone spire to the tower. The triple arched entrance and jutting gargoyles give an Early French look, whilst the chunky battered forms and stylised ironwork are typically High Victorian in treatment. Claimed to be the largest Presbyterian church in Ireland, St Enoch's had a magnificent theatre-like interior with two tiers of galleries around three sides, and four great rooflights up above. The arrangement was apparently suggested by the Reverend Hugh Hanna for whom the church was built. Tragically this double-galleried interior, unique in an Irish church, was ruined by a malicious fire in 1985.

Alongside stood St Enoch's school, also by Jackson, 1881, enlarged 1896, now destroyed.

St Enoch's Presbyterian Church

St Enoch's Presbyterian Church interior before the fire of 1985

84 **ST MATTHEW'S CHURCH OF IRELAND**, Shankill Road.
Welland and Gillespie of Dublin, 1870–2 (John Lowry & Son, builders).

A remarkable Neo-Gothic round-towered church of striking appearance on an unusual plan, basically a quatrefoil with one end expanded to form a traditional gabled west end. The compass has determined almost everything here from the plan and section to the big multi-circled west window. The exterior is a masterpiece of consumate brickwork, smooth planed and striped in red on white, whilst the open tri-apsal space of the interior with smooth coved ceilings is a real surprise in an age of dark-stained timber trussed roofs on more traditionally laid out plans. Reredos designed by Sir Thomas Graham Jackson of London, 1918; north vestry by Henry Seaver, 1933.

St Matthew's Church of Ireland: interior

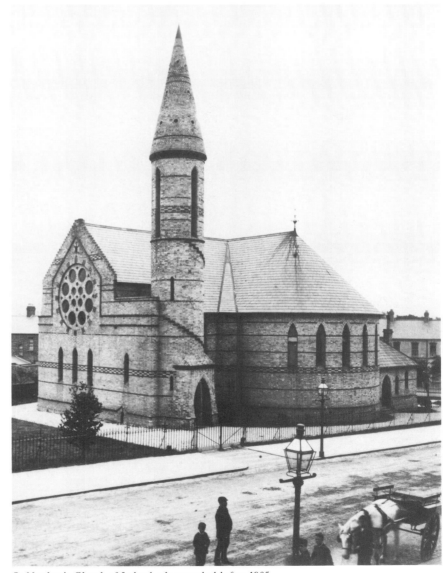

St Matthew's Church of Ireland, photographed before 1905

85 **ST JUDE'S CHURCH OF IRELAND**, Ormeau Road.
Thomas Drew, designed 1869; built 1871–3 (Fitzpatrick Brothers, builders).

The main feature of interest in this otherwise routine church is Drew's Gothic Revivalist treatment of the more usually Romanesque Round Tower type of belfry, with slated roof and lancet windows, and open arcaded topmost storey. This tower, as well as the site, was the gift of the builder William Fitzpatrick and his brothers. Church enlarged twice by Drew: the whole east side, chancel and transepts, was moved out in 1889; and the north transept gable moved out, nave gable moved out, and south side extended, 1898–9. Thus only the round tower and adjoining porch have remained in their original position. Boundary wall and gates added by Drew, 1891.

Former Synagogue, Great Victoria Street

St Jude's Church of Ireland

87 Former **SYNAGOGUE** (now an Apostolic Church), Great Victoria Street.
Francis Stirrat, 1871.

A small building with a High Victorian Gothic facade in polychrome brick and a stone plate traceried rose window, designed by the Irish partner of James Hamilton of Glasgow. The lower frontage has been spoilt by ruthless modern work. Opposite to the north, another polychrome brick facade of Italian Gothic type, the Baptist Church by William Hastings of 1864–6, has been similarly despoiled.

88 **21–25 BEDFORD STREET**.
John Boyd, 1871.

Three gabled warehouses on a curving street front in polychrome brick, each with a curious Franco-Italian arcaded oriel with imbricated roof. A High Victorian jumble by a master of the art, with ungainly brackets, hairy head keystones, rose windows and corbelled eaves course. Built for William Ferguson, a linen merchant.

23 Bedford Street

A short distance south at 35 Bedford Street is another High Victorian polychrome brick facade of varied window rhythms, built as a store for S. Boas, a fancy box manufacturer, by Lanyon, Lynn and Lanyon, 1867.

86 **WILLOWFIELD CHURCH OF IRELAND**, Woodstock Road.
Lanyon, Lynn and Lanyon, 1871–2.

A striking High Victorian Gothic church designed by John Lanyon, with bold shapes, smooth planes, polychrome brickwork and stone plate-traceried rose windows. Lanyon's original rather Continental looking belfry tower has been truncated. Nave extended by one bay and a porch added to it, by W. J. Fennell, 1900–1. The rectory on My Lady's Road was designed by John Lanyon, 1874.

Willowfield Parish Hall, opposite the church, on Woodstock Road, was by James McB. Neill, 1955.

In connection with Willowfield Church Fennell also designed the half-timbered Mission Hall on Cregagh Road at Dromore Street corner, 1910, and Willowfield National School (now Harding Memorial) alongside it, 1912; later extended by R. S. Wilshere, 1929 and 1932.

Willowfield Church of Ireland: sketch by J.J. Phillips

**89 FITZROY PRESBYTERIAN
CHURCH**, University Street.
Young and Mackenzie, 1872–4 (William
McCammond, builder).

A robust piece of Gothic Revivalism designed by Robert M. Young. The most striking
feature is the tall corner tower and spire,
detached from the church at the base but
joined higher up by a flying arcaded link to
the gallery. A good group is formed with the
school and sexton's house to the rear, all
carried out in Scrabo sandstone. Boundary
plinth and gate piers were added in 1902.

Other churches in south Belfast by the
same firm are the nicely coloured Windsor
Presbyterian, Lisburn Road and Derryvol-
gie Avenue, 1885–7, with hall and school of
1927; and the later and plainer Malone Presbyterian, Lisburn Road and Balmoral Avenue, 1898–9.

90 NEWS LETTER OFFICES, Donegall Street.
William Hastings, 1872–4.

High Victorian Gothic, with triple arcaded
windows, foliated capitals, gabled dormers
and a turret over the central entrance bay.
Built of sandstone with polished granite
columns but all has now been painted over
and the natural coloration lost. Across the
front of the first floor is a series of sculpted
medallions with portrait reliefs of celebrated
men and women, but bearing no inscriptions.

News Letter Offices

Carlisle Memorial Methodist Church

**91 CARLISLE MEMORIAL
METHODIST CHURCH** (now closed),
Carlisle Circus.
William Henry Lynn, 1872–5 (James Carli-
sle, builder).

A very good example of a Gothic Revival
Church in Early English style, excellent in
composition and in details, and well proportioned with a tower and rich spire on a really
grand scale. The magnificent gift of one man
to the community, this striking church was
built by James Carlisle in memory of his son.
Sadly it was abandoned as a church after a
century of use.

Next to the church, and superficially similar in style is the Sunday School and connec-
ting cloister, by J. J. Phillips, 1888.

Fitzroy Presbyterian Church

92 Former **ST MALACHY'S SCHOOL**, Oxford Street.
Alexander McAlister, 1874.

Run by the Christian Brothers, this two-classroomed school was designed by one of the leading Catholic architects in Belfast. A simple little gable fronted building in Italian Gothic style with arcaded windows, banded masonry and voussoirs of alternately light and dark stone. The gable roses and arcades below are quaintly unaligned.

McAlister also designed St. Mary's Catholic Hall, Bank Street, 1874–5, and St Matthew's R. C. Church, Newtownards Road, 1881–3. His most important domestic work was Trench House, St Mary's Teacher Training College, Stewartstown Road, an Italianate house with a fine hall and stairway, built for Arthur Hamill, 1880.

Former St Malachy's School

St Mark's Church of Ireland, Holywood Road, Dundela

93 **ST MARK'S CHURCH OF IRELAND**, Holywood Road.
William Butterfield of London. Nave, aisles and tower, 1876–8 (Fitzpatrick Brothers, builders); chancel, 1889–91 (H. & J. Martin, builders).

A fairly typical Butterfield church of the great English master's maturity, with an imposing exterior, its tall square belfry visible for some distance around. Scale-patterning to the tower roof, and banded walls of red Dundonald sandstone to tower and church: an eclectic mix of Continental Gothic styles with the addition of English tracery types. Butterfield's love of strong shapes and patterns is evident inside although it is disappointing that the dadoes and spandrels were left undecorated. The most noteworthy feature is the traceried arch to the baptistry beneath the tower supported on one thin colonnette.

Church gates and railings erected 1888, to Butterfield's designs, but the plain red rectory alongside was by S. P. Close, 1887. *See* pl. IX.

94 **ST PATRICK'S ROMAN CATHOLIC CHURCH**, Donegall Street.
Timothy Hevey in conjunction with **Mortimer Thompson**, 1874–7 (Collen Brothers of Portadown and Dublin, builders).

A powerful Romanesque Revival church with a striking and effective tower and spire, the front wall of the tower forming the west wall of the nave. With its rather heavy Early French detailing it is more massive than most of Hevey's works. Owing to stonework decay, much of the lower front has been refaced, its crisp-cut edges at odds with the weathered and crumbling surfaces above. The wrought-iron Celtic cross finial on the spire was made by Alfred Webb of Ballymacarrett. The Portland stone statue of St Patrick over the entrance was carved by Neill & Pearse of Dublin. They also carved the elaborate high altar. In a side chapel on the south side is a triptych of St Patrick, the Madonna, and St Bridget, painted by Sir John Lavery, but the Irish granite altar provided for it in 1919 by Sir Edwin Lutyens of London (his only Belfast work) is no longer to be seen.

St Patrick's Roman Catholic Church

95 Former **HOSPITAL FOR SICK CHILDREN** (now a Police Station), Queen Street.
Thomas Jackson and Son, 1877–8 (William McCammond, builder).

Although much darkened now this was originally a fairly bright building entirely fronted in white Scrabo sandstone. Built in the centre of what was then a very populous district of the town, the front was set back some feet from the line of adjoining buildings to gain some extra light and air. The style is a form of Early Renaissance, chosen no doubt to recall, in a modest way, the great period of hospital building in Jacobean England. The building functioned as a hospital until its much larger sucessor was built on Falls Road in 1928–32.

Former Hospital for Sick Children, Queen Street: perspective sketch of 1877

96 **LOMBARD STREET**, commercial development of 1870s.

This street of commercial development was opened up between Castle Place and Rosemary Street in the 1870s. None of the buildings is individually spctacular but together they give an idea of the scale and texture of the Mid-Victorian town.

Individual buildings which may be noted are, on the west corner with Rosemary Street, Gordon House by Thomas Jackson & Son, 1878, somewhat Scottish in feel in red sandstone with a domed corner dormer; the stuccoed Irish Temperance League building next to it by Joseph Marsh, 1877; and to the left of that a more imposing arcaded front to a five storey warehouse for Robb & Co. by William Hastings, 1874, with what looks like the hand of the Fitzpatricks at work.

On the east side is a four-storey block designed 1875, and to its right a three-storey block with attics, 1874, both by Thomas Jackson & Son.

Lombard Street: west side corner with Rosemary Street

Lombard Street: west side showing Robb's Warehouse

97 PRESBYTERIAN CHURCH, Townsend Street.
Young and Mackenzie, 1876–8 (William McCammond, builder).

Notable for its rich and effective French Romanesque triple doorways. Like so many of this firm's churches the interior is galleried round three sides. A school and sexton's house adjoin the rear.

Contemporary with this is the same firm's Westbourne Presbyterian Church, Newtownards Road, of 1877–8 with a Gothic Revivalist round tower belfry; transepts added by W. J. Fennell, 1886.

Townsend Street Presbyterian Church

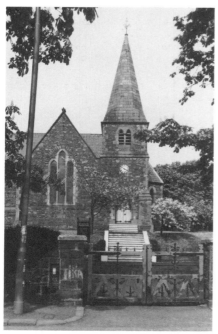

St Mark's Church of Ireland, Ballysillan, Ligoniel Road

98 ST MARK'S CHURCH OF IRELAND, Ligoniel Road.
Furnished and decorated by **James J. Phillips**, 1877–9; enlarged 1885–6.

There were three phases of building at St Mark's. The original small early Victorian Gothic Revival church of 1854, credited to Charles Lanyon but probably the work of his then assistant W. H. Lynn, was laid out with its nave gable facing the road. The original tower is still undisturbed but the church was re-oriented and enlarged in High Victorian manner with the addition in 1866 of a red stone banded nave and polygonal chancel by W. H. Lynn of Lanyon, Lynn and Lanyon. With this new work running at right angles to the original church the earlier nave then became the south transept. Finally in 1885–6 Phillips lengthened both the new nave and the north transept, built on an organ chamber, and erected the wooden baptistry screen.

Previously the chancel had been decorated to Phillips' designs, in 1877, and the gabled organ built in 1879. Much of his stencilled work to the chancel has now disappeared but the Gothic Revivalist painted dado remains, as do the elaborate wrought iron chancel rails. Probably the finest single contribution to the furnishings by Phillips is the polychrome wrought iron font cover.

The bold High Victorian iron work on the big chamfered timber gates to the church grounds was probably also by Phillips.

99 HOLY CROSS MONASTERY, Crumlin Road.
O'Neill and Byrne, 1877–81 (Robert Corry, builder).

Built of white Scrabo freestone with bands of Dundonald red, though the colour contrast is not so pronounced now. A fine open porch with columns of Newry granite and a stairway inside of white Donegal marble. The stones are thus all native but the style is imported; fittingly for the Passionist Order, it is Lombardic Romanesque. Attic storey originally dormered but the walls were later built up to form a third storey by Charles Powell of Dublin, 1930–1.

For the adjoining church of 1900–2 see separate entry.

100 ST JOSEPH'S ROMAN CATHOLIC CHURCH, Prince's Dock Street.
Timothy Hevey, completed by **Mortimer Thompson**, 1878–80 (Henry Fulton, builder).

Hevey died before building work started. In Italian Romanesque style with rather incongruous Early French details. Front built of Dungannon sandstone with red Dundonald dressings. The spire is its most effective feature. The interior consists of a nave of four bays covered by a wooden barrel ceiling with narrow aisles and a shallow sanctuary. The six statues on corbels in the nave were sculpted by John Loughlin. Behind the church in Pilot Street is the red brick parochial house by Thompson, 1879.

St Joseph's Roman Catholic Church

Holy Cross Monastery

St Malachy's School and St Joseph's Convent

101 ST MALACHY'S SCHOOL and **ST JOSEPH'S CONVENT OF MERCY,** Sussex Place.

School by **Timothy Hevey**, 1878.
Convent by **Alexander McAlister**, 1879–80 (J. & J. Guiler, builders).

A nice Gothic Revivalist group in red brick. Typically High Victorian in its treatment of the school tower, bold in form, with flat planes and crisp edges, and some banding of stonework. The school was paid for with money left by Matthew Bowen. Hevey died a few months after it opened.

102 QUEEN'S ARCADE, Donegall Place.

James F. Mackinnon, 1880.

A long shopping arcade with a glazed vault built in conjunction with George Fisher's former Castle Restaurant premises, a four-storey High Victorian frontage to Donegall Place. Some of the ornamental detail of this pavilion roofed frontage was lost when the restaurant was remodelled for Austin Reed by P. J. Wellwood of London, 1930. New shopfronts were designed for the entire arcade by Sage of London in 1932 but only a few vestiges of that stylish work remain.

Other works by Mackinnon are a largely unspoilt pair of adjoining four-storey warehouses on the east side of Donegall Street at Nos. 19–23, both designed in 1881.

103 FORTWILLIAM PARK PRESBYTERIAN CHURCH, Antrim Road.

Henry Chappell of Newtownards, 1880–5 (James Henry, builder).

An impressive High Victorian Gothic church, effectively Early French, but with some good English detail such as that of the porchway capitals. A building of two storeys, the galleried church having been built over a school-room hall. Additions to east end, including a Gothic arched covered way, designed by John MacGeagh in association with Allan Dorman, 1953.

Queen's Arcade

Fortwilliam Park Presbyterian Church

104 **BELFAST ROYAL ACADEMY**, Cliftonville Road.
Young and Mackenzie, 1878–80 (Dixon and Co., builders).

Designed in appropriate late Gothic style but given a Scottish Baronial cast by corbelled turrets and conical roofed stair towers. An original touch is the use of circular heads to the upper floor windows. This is a Late Victorian version of the Tudor Collegiate theme already seen in Belfast at Queen's College. Built of uncoursed Scrabo sandstone with tooled dressings of the same material. The date 1785 in one of the entrance arch sprandrels refers to the year the academy was inaugurated.

Belfast Royal Academy

105 **THE MULHOUSE WORKS** (in Royal Victoria Hospital grounds), Grosvenor Road.
William R. Waters, 1880.

Built for Robert Lindsay & Co. this exceptionally long thirty-one bay three-storey warehouse has a carved head keystone over each of its first floor windows. This is Waters' only work of any distinction.

106 **THE ROYAL AVENUE DEVELOPMENT** of 1880s

From Castle Place to North Street and from there at an angle to York Street a grand thoroughfare was cut through some narrow streets by the City Corporation in 1880–1. Much building opportunity was thus created over the following years. Development was controlled by a standard cornice height but the number of storeys, the materials used, and the skyline effects varied from building to building. Much of the work was in undistinguished Italianate style but at least the duller buildings gained by the coherence of the whole. Amongst them are such buildings along the east side of the avenue as that on the corner with Castle Place, designed by David Salmond in 1881; the south side of the junction with Rosemary Street, designed by Thomas Jackson and Son in 1882, and the north side by Young and Mackenzie in 1882; the north side of the junction with Lower Garfield Street designed by Young and Mackenzie in 1883; and the north side of the junction with North Street by Thomas Jackson, 1884.

A century later this coherence of the whole was ruined with some demolition on the western side. The most powerful building in the avenue, the Post Office by James Higgins Owen of Dublin 1884–6, was the chief loss in this destruction.

Some individual buildings are worthy of particular note as follows in entries 107–110.

The Mulhouse Works

Royal Avenue, looking north

107 **REFORM CLUB**, Royal Avenue.
Maxwell and Tuke of Manchester, 1883–5
(James Henry, builder).

A red sandstone building in fairly free classical style, with features mainly French in origin.

108 **NORTHERN BANK**, Royal Avenue.
John Lanyon, 1883–5.

A rather complicated composition but successfully handled, in a comparatively strict Renaissance style, if a little old fashioned for the time. Its most marked features are the two narrow end pavilions which originally had open loggias (now glazed) at the top, and projecting square oriels probably of German origin.

Reform Club, sketched c.1891

Northern Bank, Royal Avenue

109 **CENTRAL LIBRARY**, Royal Avenue.
W. H. Lynn, 1883–8 (H. & J. Martin, builders).

The result of a competition held in 1883. A very refined classical composition in Dumfries red sandstone on a black granite base. Very French in style with horizontal ground floor rustications and a rather delicately proportioned order above. Over it all is a well-treated attic, but the original pilastered chimneys have been removed. Most notable interior is the domed and Corinthian columned reference library. Bold wrought iron balustrades to the stairway made by Brawn & Co. of Birmingham.

In the next block to the north are the *Belfast Telegraph* newspaper offices, by Henry Seaver, 1886.

Central Library

110 Former **GRESHAM LIFE OFFICE** (now a shop and store), Royal Avenue. **William J. Gilliland**, 1887.

From the Gothic camp of the Queen Anne movement. A narrow gabled facade in deep toned terracotta, almost a piece of architectural cabinet making with its small intricate parts neatly fitted together.

Next door to the left, a sombre piece in Dumfries sandstone by William Fennell, 1885.

Some of Gilliland's best commercial work has been destroyed but two churches still remain: Crumlin Road Methodist, Tennent Street, 1883, and Nelson Memorial Presbyterian, Annesboro' Street, off Shankill Road, 1893. He also designed the large warehouse on the north side of Victoria Square, 1893; extended and corner turret added, 1896.

111 **ORANGE HALL**, Clifton Street. **William Batt**, 1883–5 (Dixon & Co., builders).

Three arcaded storeys of sandstone from Newtownards with Dumfries cornice, string courses and portico. A fairly ordinary design but made eye-catching by the ten feet high bronze equestrian statue (the only one in Belfast) of the triumphant figure of 1690, King William III of Orange, by Harry Hems of Exeter; unveiled November 1889. Batt also designed West Belfast Orange Hall, Shankill Road, 1897–8.

Clifton Street Orange Hall

112 **THOMPSON MEMORIAL FOUNTAIN**, Ormeau Avenue and Bedford Street. **Young and MacKenzie**, 1884–5 (Robert Corry, builder).

Built as a memorial to a local physician, Thomas Thompson of the Home of Incurables, this drinking fountain has a tall crocketed spire clustered round with spirelets. Decked out with gables, tracery and tablet flowers, it is clearly inspired by the Eleanor crosses of the late 13th century in England, but is smaller in size and less befigured. Dumfries red sandstone on a grey granite base, with basins of Aberdeen red.

Former Gresham Life Office

Thompson Memorial Fountain

Former Robinson and Cleaver Store

113 Former **ROBINSON AND CLEAVER STORE**, Donegall Square North.
Young and Mackenzie, 1886–8 (H. & J. Martin, builders).

The palatial 'Royal Irish Linen Warehouse' of the world famous firm Robinson and Cleaver. Built in that free treatment of classical style so readily termed 'Victorian'. Eye-catching and massive, it is a six storey pile with ogee copper domes. Upper floors of Scrabo sandstone from the builder's own quarries, but the ground floor faced with imported Scottish granites, also used for window colonettes throughout. Carved stonework by Harry Hems of Exeter includes swags of fruit of various countries, Donatello-like boys supporting third floor balconettes, and a series of panels with plump little children carrying flax, Irish linen and shields. The Royal Arms with those of Antrim and Belfast are carved around the corner tower, whilst about fifty life-sized heads of people from Greenland to India ornament the first floor pediments, with heroic-sized busts of Victoria and Albert, George Washington and other notables. There is also a female emerging from under a veil which was supposed to be symbolic of Australia. On the closure of the firm the interior was gutted and the fine central staircase in white marble (made by Robinson & Son of York Street) was removed.

114 **THE CRESCENT CHURCH** (originally Presbyterian), University Road.
John Bennie Wilson of Glasgow, 1885–7.

A solid looking church and hall in 14th century Gothic style, built of grey rubble with ashlar dressings. A mixture of English and French inspiration but fairly plainly treated. Most notable feature is the remarkable and beautiful tower. Almost half its height is taken up with an open belfry stage of high narrow lights crowned with a steep hipped roof.

The Crescent Church

115 **McARTHUR HALL**, Methodist College, Malone Road.
Sir Thomas Newenham Deane and Son of Dublin, 1887–91 (Robert Corry, builder).

The result of a competition with sixty entries. A beautiful piece of free Tudor design picturesquely grouped and with some interesting details around the doorway. Built as a hall of residence for girls at the Methodist College. Good features inside include the late Gothic-style hooded fireplace in the corridor and the Elizabethan-style plastered ceiling to the library. The big hammer beamed dining hall has two fine carved wooden fireplace surrounds, one inscribed 'C. Cambi, Scolpi, Siena', the other 'T.M. Deane Archt, Dublino'. That was the son in the firm, Thomas Manley Deane.

McArthur Hall

116 48 & 50 FOUNTAIN STREET.
Godfrey Ferguson, 1888.

Built as a spirit warehouse for Lyle and Kinahan. A quaint brickwork gable, very Dutch in form, with a typical mixture of Queen Anne Revival motifs – modelled pilasters, cusped tracery windows, stepped gable copings and a miniature pediment on top. Ferguson had travelled in Northern Europe, and in the seventies worked in London for two men at the forefront of the Queen Anne Revival, J. J. Stevenson and E. R. Robson, before returning to Belfast.

117 QUEEN'S BRIDGE
Original structure by **Charles Lanyon** and **John Frazer**, 1840–43; widened by **J. C. Bretland**, 1885–6.

The original bridge was a massive and handsome five arched granite affair. Its plain appearance was very much altered when Bretland added footpaths cantilevered out from the sides on clusters of stumpy columns with big Early French capitals. The cast-iron fish-ornamented lamp standards installed in this widening scheme were made by George Smith's 'Sun Foundry' of Glasgow.

118 ALBERT BRIDGE
J. C. Bretland, 1888–90 (Robert Corry, builder).

Designed in 1886 following the collapse of the old Albert Bridge that year. Built of granite with three cast-iron arches, each containing eleven arched ribs of 85 ft span.

Bretland came to Belfast from Nottingham in 1867 to become assistant to the borough surveyor, and then took over that office in 1884. He was responsible for many improvements in the city during the 1880s such as the stone and concrete river wall along the tidal course of the River Lagan; the laying out of several parks such as Woodvale and Alexandra; the design of pumping stations such as that at Duncrue Street; and the forming of several new streets, most notably Royal Avenue.

48 & 50 Fountain Street

Queen's Bridge

Albert Bridge

119 GAS WORKS OFFICES, Ormeau Road.
Robert Watt, 1887–8.

Designed by a leading local architect and not by the manager of the works as popularly supposed, this long red brick range in Queen Anne style has a very fine oak stairway and tiled entrance hall near its north end. Balusters, pilasters, pediments, freizes and dados in the hall are all made of coloured ceramic and together make one of the most sumptuous late Victorian interiors in Ulster. Along the outside wall is a good series of unglazed terracotta panels of rich Renaissance ornament. The round clock tower is now somewhat changed from the original: a copper spire has replaced the slated roof and wrought iron railings have replaced the pierced stone balustrade. At the southernmost end of the site is the massive gabled Retort House, 1890–1, in red brick with a rich Renaissance terracotta frieze and sandstone carved Belfast arms in the pediment facing Ormeau Road. Also by Watt, but out of view, is the domed Middle Section Meter House, 1887, also derelict. Elsewhere in the city Watt was architect for Offices for the Ropeworks on Newtownards Road, 1889, and the former Mooney's Public House with its curved brick frontage to Arthur Square, 1888, but his coloured ceramics there have now disappeared. *See* pl. X.

Gas Works Offices

Gas Works Offices clock tower

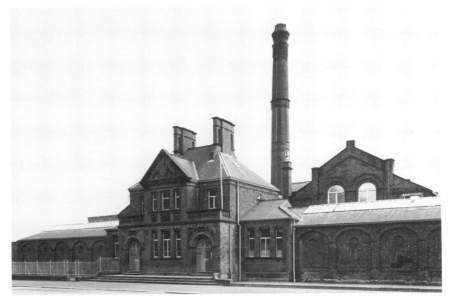

Public Baths, Ormeau Avenue

120 **PUBLIC BATHS**, Ormeau Avenue. **Robert Watt**, 1887–9.

Tall narrow windows and steep pediment; arched chimneys and carved Renaissance ornament; modelled brickwork and squat balusters – these are characteristic of the Queen Anne Revival style though here very sombrely handled. Note the carvings of mermaids looking at their reflection in handmirrors over one of the entrances.

121 **PUBLIC BATHS**, Templemore Avenue. **Robert Watt**, 1891–3.

A virtually intact survival of the Victorian age. Fairly similar in general layout to Ormeau Baths but more crisply and simply detailed. A central two-storey administration block leads off to long low ranges of baths with large gabled blocks behind containing the 1st and 2nd class pools. Between these is the boiler house with its tall brick chimney.

Public Baths, Templemore Avenue

54

122 **ST GEORGE'S MARKET**, May Street and East Bridge Street.
J. C. Bretland, 1890–6

Three pedimented Roman triumphal arch motifs alternate with a minor variation on the same theme. In red brick with sandstone dressings it all makes for handsome street facades which dignify an otherwise utilitarian structure. Light and spacious interiors with glazed roofs carried on cast-iron columns made by Ritchie, Hart & Co. of Belfast. Built in portions over a six year period to house the sale of butter, eggs and poultry until, on eventual completion, it also became the fruit market.

St George's Market

123 **THE FISH MARKET**, Oxford Street.
J. C. Bretland, 1896.

A variant of the Roman triumphal arch motif with double pilasters introduced and an effective iron grille. It makes for a handsome entrance to the still functioning Fish Market. Along with the gateways to St George's Market opposite, it maintains the identity of the markets area in a very grand way.

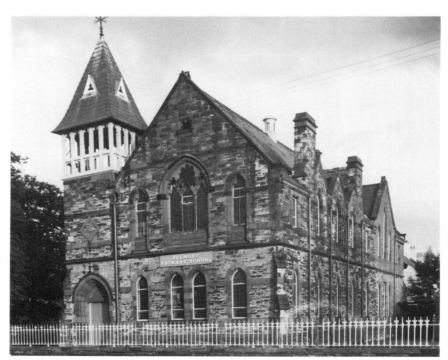

Belmont Primary School

124 **BELMONT PRIMARY SCHOOL**, Belmont Road.
Vincent Craig, 1890–2 (Dixon & Campbell, builders).

An endearing little Gothic Revivalist school in buff sandstone with red dressings and an open belfried tower. Erected as a memorial to Mrs Mary Ferguson of Sydenham. Extended to the rear by Thomas Houston, 1909–10.

A short way to the north on Sydenham Avenue is Belmont Presbyterian Church (originally by W. J. Barre, 1860–1) where Craig extended the nave and added a tall tower in 1898–1900.

125 **ST JOHN'S PRESBYTERIAN CHURCH**, Ormeau Road.
Vincent Craig, 1890–2 (Robert Corry, builder).

Craig was a pupil of W. H. Lynn but left him in 1889 so this is one of his first jobs on his own. Gothic Revival of a rather episcopalian type it seems to owe something to Lynn in compositional terms but the polygonal bays pushed out from flat wall planes already suggest the quirky direction Craig's later work would take. Interesting detail throughout.

In front of the church, an unusual Ist World War memorial, ogee domed with cusped panels.

The Fish Market

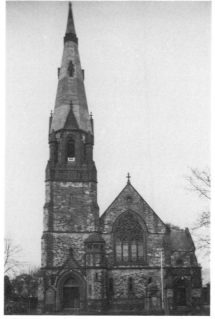

St John's Presbyterian Church

126 JENNYMOUNT MILL EXTEN-SION, North Derby Street.
John Lanyon, 1891.

A massive towering seven-storey brick block, like an Italian medieval palazzo with its battered base and its corbel course. The construction is of cast iron columns with fireproof floors of brick arches and concrete laid over.

John Lanyon's Tower Buildings of 1893 in Ormeau Avenue next to the public baths were similar in style but were maliciously destroyed in the 1970s.

Harbour Office: main front

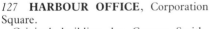

Jennymount Mill Extension

Harbour Office: perspective view of George Smith's original building

127 HARBOUR OFFICE, Corporation Square.

Original building by George Smith, 1852–4; enlarged by **W. H. Lynn**, 1891–5 (H. & J. Martin, builders).

The earlier office by George Smith was a two storeyed Renaissance palazzo entirely of polished freestone with a Doric portico and a clock tower with belfry. Its seaward facade still stands intact, but its entrance front is two thirds absorbed into Lynn's large and well massed later building. It is mainly of two storeys too but the blocks forming the wings of its main front have prominent attics. There are similarities with Lynn's Public Library but here the detail is Italian rather than French. The broad and deep Ionic portico is nicely handled. Inside is a good series of interiors. The most notable are the entrance hallway furnished with a fine pair of Coalbrookdale lamp standards; the grand staircase and first floor lobby; and the magnificent Corinthian columned Public Hall with a vaulted ceiling and heraldic stained glass in the clerestorey lunettes. *See* pl. XIII.

Harbour Office: interior of the Public Hall

128 **CAMPBELL COLLEGE**, Belmont Road.
W. H. Lynn, 1892–4 (Henry Laverty & Son, builders).

The tower-form gatelodge is a nice introduction to the larger towered main building, a picturesquely grouped exercise in Tudor Revivalism, reserved in style and refined in detail. Memorable galleried main hall with rose window and hammer beam roof. On one wall of the hall is a fine Late Gothic style 1st World War memorial, designed by James Reid Young of Young and MacKenzie, executed by Henry Laverty & Sons, and incorporating four good figure sculptures by Rosamond Praeger of Holywood, Co. Down.

Campbell College

Campbell College: War Memorial

Dunville Fountain

129 **DUNVILLE FOUNTAIN**,
Dunville Park, Falls Road.
1892.

Although now dried up and very badly vandalised this is still an astonishing piece of ceramic work almost all in buff terracotta. So similar to the French Renaissance style Victoria Fountain in Glasgow, 1888, that it must surely also be by Messrs. Doulton of Lambeth, and probably also the design of their staff artist A. E. Pearce. The figures at the top have been all but knocked off but the rich Renaissance ornament, masks and the like, is still to be seen. Nice panels of aquatic life in relief near the base. This once pretty park was entirely paid for and presented to the city by Robert G. Dunville of distilling fame.

130 **ST JOHN'S CHURCH OF IRELAND**, Malone Road.
Henry Seaver, 1893–5; nave not built until 1905 (W. J. Campbell & Son, builder).

A pleasant late Victorian church in Gothic style whose tower was never finished. Worth a visit on account of its Irish stained glass windows. Those to note are *St Patrick* in the north transept by Katherine O'Brien of Dublin, 1938; 'Pro Patria' in the north side of the nave by William McBride of Dublin, 1918, and the Ferguson and Ireland memorial windows on the south side which also look like McBride's work; the Wheeler Memorial window, a masterpiece on the theme of 'The Leaves of the Tree were for the Healing of the Nations', on the north side, by Wilhelmina Geddes of Dublin, 1919–20; the rose window of 'Symbols' in the west gable, to the memory of the architect of the church, *St Brigid* in the west porch, and *St Columba* in the north transept, all by Evie Hone of Dublin, 1948. Geddes and Hone were figures of international importance. Of local interest are windows by Ward & Partners of Belfast: one in the west porch, *St Comgall* in the north transept, and *Faith*, *Hope* and *Charity* in the south transept. These last three were designed by William Douglas, 1906.

St John's Church of Ireland

131 **BANK OF IRELAND** (formerly National Bank), High Street.
William Batt, 1893–7 (H. & J. Martin, builders).

A lofty fireproof concrete block clad in red brick and buff terracotta (now sadly over-painted), and crowned with a Mansard roof and turrets. Designed in a kind of Franco-Flemish Renaissance style but the whole ground floor has been ruthlessly modernised. Of James Edgar Winter's reputedly fine carved oak doors there now remains no trace.

Imperial Buildings to the right was by W. J. Gilliland, 1906; re-erected from the second floor up after damage in the blitz of 1941, but with some details omitted.

132 **TRUSTEE SAVINGS BANK** (originally Dunville's Offices), Arthur Street.
Vincent Craig, 1894.

A two storeyed Italian Renaissance-style palazzo with a pediment sitting rather oddly on top seeming to need some breaks in the facade below with which to relate. A simple but substantial grey granite front tastefully left unpolished. Shallow domed interior with ornamental plasterwork.

133 **GALLAHER'S TOBACCO FACTORY**, York Street.
Samuel Stevenson, 1894 with various additions.

The five storey block on Earl Street corner and the gabled range to its right came first, in 1894, while much of the rest was built up over the early 1900s. The big long ranges toward the rear were added in the 1930s by Samuel Stevenson and Sons. Lots of red brick but little of interest except for three carved heads on the entrance front.

Nearby on York Street and Henry Street are the big blocky brick masses of the former York Street Flax Spinning Company warehouses, reconstructed after war damage by Samuel Stevenson and Sons, 1947.

134 **GRAND OPERA HOUSE**, Great Victoria Street.
Frank Matcham of London, 1894–5 (H. & J. Martin, builders).

Designed by the leading theatre architect of his day in a deliberately eye-catching way. A bizarre jumble of Renaissance elements with onion shaped ventilator domes placed on top. The oriental suggestion here is compounded inside where Indian motifs, including elephant heads, are brought into play in a lavish and rather Baroque ensemble.

Restored, 1976–80, by Robert McKinstry who added the crush bar over the entrance. *See* pl. XII.

Bank of Ireland, High Street

Trustee Savings Bank, Aurthur Street

Gallaher's Tobacco Factory

Grand Opera House

58

135 ALL SOULS NON-SUBSCRIBING PRESBYTERIAN CHURCH, Elmwood Avenue.
Walter Planck of London, 1895–6 (James Henry, builder).

A very English looking church with its open oak porch and its rather dumpy tower modelled on that of Croyland Abbey in Lincolnshire. Of Scrabo stone with Doulting dressings, with good late fourteenth century detail. The interior is very impressive due to the continuous walls and roof over the nave and chancel with big traceried windows at each end. All in all an exquisite building; a gem of late Victorian church architecture. The memorial board at the west end of the nave was illuminated by Charles Braithwaite, 1908.

Behind the church is the 'Arts and Crafts' English Domestic Revival-style Church Hall by W. J. Gilliland, 1908.

Mater Hospital

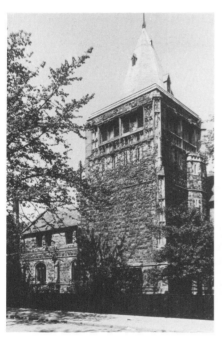
All Souls Church

Mater Hospital: roof garden, photographed around 1905

136 MATER HOSPITAL, Crumlin Road.
William J. Fennell, 1895–1900 (H. Laverty & Sons, builders).

Laid out on the pavilion plan whereby good natural ventilation was promoted between windows on opposite sides of tall narrow buildings. The chief interest, however, of this fairly dull Tudoresque red brick building lies in the roof construction of the wards. Pitched roofs were at first intended for all the blocks but Fennell eventually chose for the wards flat roofs covered with Vulcanite which were then laid out as gardens. Those roofs are still flat but the beds of grass have been cleared away. To the rear of the administration block is the galleried chapel, in late Gothic style.

Low extensions to the west next to the gaol, by Young and MacKenzie, 1933. Nearby, to the east, the Nurses Home by Frank McArdle, 1931.

Mater Hospital: interior of chapel

Ballynafeigh Methodist Church: Alfred Forman's original perspective drawing

137 BALLYNAFEIGH METHODIST CHURCH, Ormeau Road.
Forman and Aston, 1897–9 (Young and Dickson, builders).

Although the special charm of its exterior has been all but destroyed the interior is still a delight, theatre-like with a gallery curving round three sides and fretted arcades in the timber trusses; clearly the work of Alfred Forman. Laid out on an unusual rather centralised plan with diagonal axes; empha-tically non-conformist. Designed in an almost indeterminate style described at the time as "an adaptation of American Romanesque". A jumble of Renaissance, Romanesque and Gothic design, the best single label would be Queen Anne Revival. The exterior was originally a very striking sight but its impact has been diminished over the years. The spire, fleche, and finials were removed at some stage and now the brick walls have been all painted over.

Ballynafeigh Methodist Church: interior

Houses at corner of Wellington Park and Lisburn Road

138 HOUSES AT CORNER OF WELLINGTON PARK AND LISBURN ROAD.
Forman and Aston, 1897.

A big swaggering Queen Anne style house on the corner with Lisburn Road dominates this attractive (though partly spoilt) half-timbered terrace. Big oversailing gables and Tuscan columned bays, with some quirky details like the 'eyebrow dormer' and the waisted columns to the porch.

Most of Alfred Forman's other work is to be found in Londonderry.

139 **THE CITY HALL**, Donegall Square.

Alfred Brumwell Thomas of London, 1896–1906 (H. & J. Martin, builders).

A magnificent building, one of the most important examples of the Baroque Revival anywhere in the British Isles. A perfect expression of the prosperity and civic pride of the city at the turn of the century. Foundation stone laid 1898. The design of Messrs. E. Thomas and Son was chosen from a field of 51 entries in the competition of 1896. Assessors were Alfred Waterhouse RA, President of the RIBA, and J. C. Bretland, City Surveyor.

Quadrangular in form with an internal courtyard, and faced with Portland stone throughout. Three storeyed along the south and west sides where the departmental offices were located, but only two storeyed along the north and east where the reception rooms and council chamber occupy the lofty upper floor.

Quite a compendium of English 17th and 18th century classicism, with a special debt to London. A Neo-Palladian wall treatment, with an Ionic order carried on a rusticated ground floor; lots of Gibbsian detail; and homage to Wren in the general domed concept. The great central dome is inspired by those of St. Paul's Cathedral and Greenwich Hospital, whilst the smaller corner cupolas are based on the twin west towers of St. Paul's. The little circular porch to the east is clearly derived from Gibbs's St. Mary le Strand, but the domed porte-cochere outside the main entrance seems to have no real precedent. The pediment on the main facade is crammed with a vigorous figure group representing 'Hibernia bearing the torch of knowledge, encouraging and promoting the commerce and arts of the city'. It is possibly the finest piece of architectural sculpture in Belfast. Designed by Frederick W. Pomeroy RA of London and executed by him along with James Edgar Winter of Belfast.

Inside, a fine series of rooms and spaces, with some lavish use of imported marbles. The black and white paved Grand Entrance Hall, with walls of Pavonazzo and Brescia marbles, leads to the Grand Staircase of double return arrangement lit by a series of Venetian windows, carried out in the same Italian marbles with addition of Carrara. To this array of Italian marbles is added green Cippalino from Greece in the colonnade and screens of the First Floor Landing. Towering over this and open to view from the entrance hall through the Rotunda, is the great dome with its Whispering Gallery, peristyle and lantern. This is one of the grandest architectural spaces in Ireland. The dome is of double construction, with an outer dome covered in copper and a smaller inner one constructed of steel with decorative plaster attached.

En suite on the first floor are the exedrae-ended Ionic columned Reception Room, the dome ceilinged Banqueting Hall, and the oak wainscotted and galleried Council Chamber. Its seats are laid out on the House of Commons model with a central gangway, but the general feel is of a Wren church interior. Excellent carved oak screen and Lord Mayor's chair on a dais, carved in the manner of Grinling Gibbons by Purdy and Millard of Belfast. The Corinthian columned Great Hall to the east was destroyed in the Blitz of 1941, but rebuilt by 1952 omitting the ceiling mouldings. The grand double return East Staircase with arcaded colonnade to the landing leads to the East Entrance Hall below. Simply treated surfaces but an interesting spatial arrangement of flat saucer domed compartments marked off by coupled columns.

Throughout these interiors the quality of material and workmanship is superb. Marble work was by Farmer & Brindley of London, and plasterwork by George Rome & Co. of Glasgow. Stained glass windows in principal rooms designed and made by Ward & Partners; leaded lights to ground floor and first floor landings and peristyle of dome, made by Campbell Brothers to the designs of A. B. Thomas.

Numerous paintings and sculptures furnish the interior. In the north tympanum below the dome, a mural representing the life and history of the city by John Luke, 1951. Facing it on the main landing, a bronze statue of the Earl of Belfast by Patrick MacDowell RA, 1855. In the octagonal vestibule off the grand entrance hall is MacDowell's masterpiece, the exquisite marble group to the memory of the Earl of Belfast, originally in Belfast Castle Chapel. It is one of the finest Victorian figure groups in the British Isles.

In the grounds around the City Hall are a number of memorials. To the north side in front of the *porte-cochere*, the impressive though ill-sited marble Statue of Queen Victoria with bronze supporting figures of Shipbuilding and Spinning by Sir Thomas Brock RA, of London, 1903. Beyond it in the centre of the main gateway is the American Forces Monument, a short stone column designed by T. F. O. Rippingham to commemorate the Americans dissembarking here in 1942; to the east side, the evocative Titanic Memorial by Brock to commemorate the loss of the great ship in 1912, and the Royal Irish Rifles South African War Memorial modelled by Sydney March of London and cast by Elkington & Co., 1905.

To the west side is the **Memorial to the First Marquis of Dufferin**, a bronze figure under a stone canopy with bronze supporting figures representing Canada and India. Designed by A. B. Thomas; executed by F. W. Pomeroy, 1906. In the Garden of Remembrance is the **Belfast War Memorial**, a Portland stone cenotaph in front of a curved colonnade of paired plain shafts with 'Tower of the Winds' capitals, by Sir Alfred Brumwell Thomas, 1925–7 (W. J. Campbell & Son, builders).

Thomas was knighted in 1906. After his success at Belfast he continued to win competitions for town halls, building three others, all in England, at Stockport, Clacton, and Woolwich.

See frontispiece and pl. XV.

Thomas's sketch of east porch

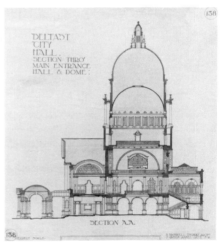

Original proposal for main entrance and dome

Council Chamber in 1906

East Staircase in 1906

The Dufferin Memorial

The City Hall: view from south-west showing Belfast War Memorial

61

62

140 SCOTTISH PROVIDENT INSTITUTION, Donegall Square West.
Young and Mackenzie, 1897–1902 (Robert Corry, builder).

A magnificent pile of Giffnock sandstone in Renaissance style enlivened with more than a touch of Free Baroque in the shallow bowed central bay and the octagonal corner cupolas. The attached order to the upper floors also helps to relieve the monotony of repetitive office windows. Much ornamental stone carving by Purdy and Millard including panels of the leading industries of Belfast of the time – printing, weaving, shipbuilding and rope-making – around the central bay. Elsewhere, lions heads and drapery abound. Around the Scottish Provident's own portion of the building on the corner with Wellington Place, are carved female heads of England, India, Canada, Sudan, Erin and Scotland. The building was erected in two sections; the first part at the Wellington Place end starting in 1897, the rest including the curved bay following in 1899.

The Crown Bar

Scottish Provident Institution

141 THE CROWN BAR, Great Victoria Street.
E. & J. Byrne, 1885 and 1898.

The Corinthian pilastered upper facade of the Crown (originally the Ulster Railway Hotel) dates from 1839–40 but its celebrated ground floor public house took its present form much later in the century. Emphatically Late Victorian in style and fabric it is one of the finest of its period in the whole of the British Isles. The popular myth is that it was designed by the publican's son; it was actually the work of E. and J. Byrne, a local firm of architects. Their remodelling work for Patrick Flannigan at The Crown was done at two different dates. The interior with its famous snugs was built in 1885, whilst the faience front with the two-columned porch was added in 1898.

Two doors away the plain pilastered Robinson's Bar (originally the Dublin and Armagh Hotel) dates originally from 1846.
See pl. XI.

The Crown Bar: interior

142 Former **KIRKER, GREER & CO. WAREHOUSE** (now the Education Office), Academy Street.
Samuel Stevenson, 1899–1901.

Formerly lost in the small streets off York Street but now clearly seen from the new roadway sweeping past. Red brick with pavilion roofed towers. Built as a warehouse for an aerated water manufacturer.

Stevenson was also architect for the large towered and turretted Co-operative Society stores on York Street nearby, built between 1911 and 1922; it has been completely obscured by modern cladding. Still to be seen is the large extension built for the Co-op on the next block to the south on York Street, in red brick with Portland stone dressings, 1930–1.

Former Kirker, Greer & Co. Warehouse

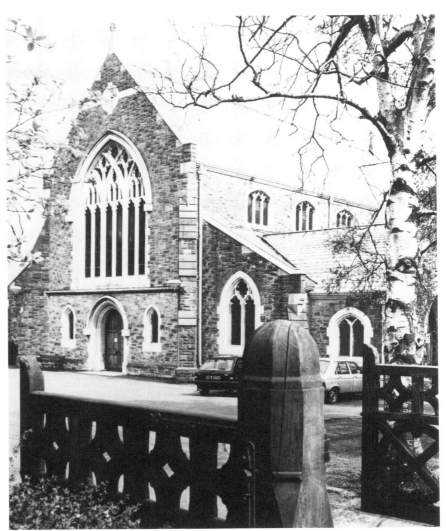

St Peter's Church of Ireland

143 **ST PETER'S CHURCH OF IRELAND**, Antrim Road.
Samuel P. Close, 1898–1900 (Henry Laverty & Sons, builders).
Western end completed by **Richard M. Close**, 1932–3.

A Late Victorian Gothic Revival church of Scrabo sandstone with Giffnock dressings, in a blend of Decorated and Perpendicular styles. A tall tower was intended for the north-west corner but was not built. Interesting interior details and furnishings. Some Irish Revivalism apparent here and there. The east window of the south transept is based on tracery at Culfeightrin Old Church; a south window of the chancel is based on the east window from Devenish Island (now in the parish church at Monea, Co. Fermanagh); and label stops in the transepts are carved with interlacing Celtic beasts derived from panels of the Clogher Cross. They spell out 'DEUS' at upper level and 'AMEN' lower down.

A rare chancel reredos in unglazed terracotta by the celebrated Victorian ceramic sculptor George Tinworth of Doulton's of Lambeth, depicts 'The Women at the Sepulchre' or 'The Empty Tomb' as it is sometimes known. Side chapel reredos of 'The Ascension into Heaven' in alabaster

St Peter's Church of Ireland: the reredos

framed with Derbyshire marble, by Morris Harding RHA, 1932. Angel Font in the bapistry, in French Portland stone on a Connemara marble base, also carved by Harding, 1932.

144 FISHERWICK PRESBYTERIAN CHURCH, Malone Road.
Samuel P. Close, 1898–1901 (Robert Corry, builder).

A landmark on the Malone Road this sandstone church closes the vista along Eglantine Avenue very effectively. Gothic Revival with fifteenth century Perpendicular tracery but a fourteenth century type spire, and a Scottish flavour to the conically roofed circular porches to the rear. Inside the front porch are three earlier Victorian classical memorials brought here from the old church in Fisherwick Place (demolished 1898). Stained glass windows in the apse were by Ward & Partners, and W. J. Douglas & Sons; and in the west gable by Clokey & Co., 1956.

Musgrave Hall to the rear along Chlorine Gardens was by R. Ferguson, 1923–4.

Close also designed St Patrick's Church of Ireland, Newtownards Road, 1891–3 (largely rebuilt 1952 after air raid damage in 1941); St Columba's Church of Ireland, King's Road, 1896; St Mary Magdalene Church of Ireland, Donegall Pass, 1899; and St Nicholas's Church of Ireland, Lisburn Road, 1899.

Clonard Monastery

Fisherwick Presbyterian Church

145 CLONARD MONASTERY, Clonard Gardens.
J. J. McDonnell, 1898–1900 (W. J. Campbell & Son, builders).

A large red brick Gothic Revival building with sandstone dressings, four storeyed, its attic with a mansard roof and dormers. Above the entrance a statue of the Redeemer with the arms of Pope Leo XIII and the Congregation of the Most Holy Redeemer. The tympana of the ground floor windows are carved with Emblems of the Passion. For the adjoining church of 1908–11 see separate entry.

Roman Catholic Church of The Most Holy Redeemer and Clonard Monastery

146 ROMAN CATHOLIC CHURCH OF THE MOST HOLY REDEEMER, Clonard Gardens.
J. J. McDonnell, 1908–11 (Naughton Brothers, builders).

McDonnell's ecclesiastical masterpiece. Sketch plans of 1897 for a Romanesque style church were set aside for this fine Gothic design. Of Early French type with bar traceried rose window and triple portals. Very rich interior, High Victorian in feel despite the late date. Highly ornamented main and side altars with mandorlas, designed by Henry Berghman CSSR, carved by Davis of Cork. Altar of St Joseph designed by McDonnell, added 1923. Along the nave walls are striking mosaics by Gabriel Loire of Chartres, 1960–1. The symbols in the clerestorey and the scenes in the spandrels illustrate the Story of the Redemption: on the north side, from the Old Testament; on the south side, from the New Testament.

Other churches by McDonnell are St Paul's, Falls Road, 1884 and St Vincent de Paul, Ligoniel Road, *c*.1897. He also designed the *Irish News* office, Donegall Street, 1905.

Holy Redeemer Church: interior

147 **THE BANK BUILDINGS**, Castle Place.
W. H. Lynn, 1899–1900 (James Henry & Sons, builders).

An ungainly looking stone clad brute in a heavy classical mode. Not the pioneering steel framed structure that has been sometimes claimed; rather it is in the conventional manner of the time with cast iron piers inside. Built of red Dumfries sandstone with a giant order of Corinthian columns in polished granite, each shaft weighing 7 tons. In the pedimented dormer is one of the then-novel patent electric clocks made locally by Sharman D. Neill.

Although this front portion of the Bank Buildings was not designed and built until the turn of the century its general treatment had been determined more than a decade earlier when Lynn had started rebuilding part of the old premises to the rear of the site, between Bank Lane and Castle Street, in 1885, in Dumfries stone with giant pilasters. He continued building in portions until all but this front block to Castle Place, seven bays deep, had been rebuilt in the same manner (James Henry was builder for all the work).

The very modern extension westwards on Castle Street was by Hobart and Heron, 1952.

On the other corner of Castle Street on Donegall Place is the five-storey Anderson & McAuley's store by Young and Mackenzie, 1895. Next door to it is the former Lindsay Brothers' warehouse by Robert Watt, 1877, a four-storey classical frontage now missing its central pediment.

148 **OCEAN BUILDINGS**, Donegall Square East.
Young and Mackenzie, 1899–1902.

The name comes from the original occupants, the Ocean Accident Guarantee Corporation. An embattled and gabled red sandstone pile overlaid with oriels and Late Gothic detail, the result no doubt of a conscious desire to look different from the other big office across the square. Some fine animal carvings by James Edgar Winter. Winter was also used by Young and Mackenzie to carve the Belfast arms on their Fire Brigade Stations at Crumlin Road 1902, and Albertbridge Road, 1903.

149 **COLLEGE OF TECHNOLOGY**, College Square East.
Samuel Stevenson, 1900–7 (W. J. Campbell & Son, builders).

A much reviled building on account of its unfortunate siting, whereby it masks part of the Academical Institution's facade. A fairly dull Baroque Revival design in Portland stone based on William Young's War Office in Whitehall (1898–1906), but the corner turrets do give a splendid focus along Great Victoria Street.

A much smaller building by Stevenson is the Dutch or Flemish gabled bow-windowed shop front at 51 Donegall Place bearing the date 1907.

The Bank Buildings

Ocean Buildings

College of Technology: front doorway

College of Technology

150 **PRESBYTERIAN ASSEMBLY BUILDINGS**, Fisherwick Place.
Young and Mackenzie, 1900–5 (Robert Corry, builder).

Young and Mackenzie were appointed to design this, the headquarters of the Presbyterian Church in Ireland, in controversial circumstances after an abortive competition. It was Robert Young himself who had originally drawn up almost impossible conditions with a cost limit of £30,000; his own firm then spent over £70,000 on the building. A rather heavy looking sandstone building in Tudor style with a welter of English late Gothic detail. Scottish overtones in the corbelled turrets and the big crown spire on the bell tower. In the main entrance spandrels the carved spiral ornament and zoomorphic interlace is a rare instance of Celtic Revivalism on a Belfast street front. Stone carving around entrances and to ground storey, by James Edgar Winter; to rest of exterior, by Purdy and Millard.

Inside, the large D-shaped Assembly Hall in stone and oak is one of the most impressive interiors in Belfast: arcaded, with two tiers of galleries and a great oblong roof-light with coloured glass of art nouveau pattern. This glass and the fine Barkley Memorial window in the Minor Hall were executed by Ward and Partners, 1905. Interior carved work by J. E. Winter includes a fine sculptured relief portrait of John Knox in the corridor which encircles the central Assembly Hall.

The turret clock was one of the most important erected in the British Isles at the time, it being the first occasion when electricity was employed to drive the clock and the chiming and carillon parts. It was devised and made by Sharman D. Neill.

Across Howard Street is the Presbyterian War Memorial Hostel by Young and Mackenzie, 1922–5 (F. B. McKee, builder), next to the former Fulton's Warehouse on corner of Great Victoria Street, by Young and Mackenzie, 1901.
See pl. XIV.

Presbyterian Assembly Buildings

Presbyterian Assembly Buildings: roof light of Assembly Hall

151 **ROYAL VICTORIA HOSPITAL**, Grosvenor Road.

Henman and Cooper of Birmingham, 1900–3 (McLaughlin & Harvey, builders).

Erected by public subscriptions organised and collected by Lord and Lady Pirrie.

A building of international renown and a revolution in hospital design. The conventional pavilion plan normally used in hospital design of the time was here set aside for a new arrangement where wards were placed compactly side by side, wall to wall, to get full advantage from the Plenum system of forced ventilation which was employed. This plan for wards, one storeyed throughout, with a basement used for air ducts, was perfectly adapted to the environmental system employed. The coconut fibre screens to clean the in-drawn air can still be seen in the Fan House. The two 10' diameter fans or air propellors to force the air on through the ducts were manufactured by Davidson's Sirocco Engineering Works. Very much a modern building despite the 'Wrenaissance' styling, it appears to be the first one anywhere to have been air conditioned for human comfort. William Henman was appointed in 1898; the design must date from that year or the next although building did not begin until 1900. Henry Lea was Consulting Engineer.

Stained glass and leaded lights designed by W. J. Douglas of Ward & Partners.

Bronze statue of Queen Victoria, originally placed over main entrance but now in front of courtyard, by J. Wenlock Rollins of Chelsea.

Numerous additions to the hospital by Young and Mackenzie include the Musgrave Memorial building which connects the east and west wings of the original adminstrative building thus turning the original open court to Grosvenor Road into a quadrangle, 1925; a neat little Surgical Clinical Theatre to augment the extern department, 1925; a Pathological Department with octagonal post mortem room next to the mortuary, at the east end, 1925; three more wards at the north-west end, 1925; and the whole multi-gabled end wall of the entire ward block moved out with verandah added, 1936. They also built the King Edward building on the corner of Grosvenor and Falls Road, 1914, and the Queen's University Institute of Pathology to the east of the hospital, 1933.

Royal Victoria Hospital: Henman's original drawing for entrance front

Royal Victoria Hospital: south side of ward block as first built

152 Former **MURPHY AND STEVENSON'S FACTORY**, Linen Hall Street.
Young and Mackenzie, 1900.

The later Victorian and Edwardian warehouses and factories are often very dreary and dull, but this one is rather impressive with its curved stair turrets to each end and its powerful main entrance: a somewhat Vanburghian affair, rugged and mannered, with obelisks on balls.

Former Murphy and Stevenson's Factory

Royal Victoria Hospital: view over wards

153 **HOLY CROSS ROMAN CATHO-LIC CHURCH**, Crumlin Road.
Doolin, Butler and Donnelly of Dublin, 1900–2 (James Henry & Sons, builders).

Lombardic Romanesque in general style like the earlier monastery to which it is attached. Its twin towered front is a landmark in west Belfast. The large tympanum carving representing the 'Taking Down from the Cross' was carved by James Ovens, of Dublin and Preston, who also was responsible for other exterior work. Highly decorated interior with ceiling and sanctuary walls painted by Brother Mark, marble mosaic work by J. F. Ebner of London, and ceramic mosaics by Craven, Dunnill & Co. of Jackfield. Nave and other capitals were carved by local men Thompson and Copeland. Unusual pulpit in Renaissance style with fine inlaid work. To the north side is the Lady Chapel with a rather classically detailed front, a neat little building with zoomorphic capitals and bas relief roundels, designed by Rudolf Butler who took control of the scheme when Walter Doolin died in 1900. Corresponding side chapel added to south by W. D. Bready, 1961.

To the north of the church on corner with Woodvale Road is the former Holy Cross School, Ardoyne, by W. J. Moore, 1913.

Holy Cross Roman Catholic Church

154 **MURRAY'S TOBACCO FACTORY**, Linfield Street.
Watt and Tulloch, 1900.

The practice of Robert Graeme Watt was given extra zest when he was joined in partnership by Frederick Tulloch from London in 1895. Watt's earlier plain red brick Queen Anne style then gave way to stripey stonework enlivened with quirky details. The pagoda-like roofs, miniature columns, and elongated keystones on this building are all characteristic of the younger man's work.

Tulloch also designed East Bridge Street Power Station, 1898, but it has now gone.

155 **STATE BUILDINGS**, Arthur Street.
Watt and Tulloch, 1902.

With a top-floor loggia and effective use of the 'Ipswich oriel', Watt and Tulloch here combine elements of various Renaissance styles.

The fine Art Deco chromium shop fronts and entrance porch inserted by Samuel Stevenson and Sons in 1932 have recently been removed.

Murray's Tobacco Factory

State Buildings

PLATE XI. *The Crown Bar. Interior.* See *141*.

PLATE XII.   *Grand Opera House. The auditorium. See 134.*

PLATE XIII.   *Harbour Office. The first floor lobby.* See *127*.

PLATE XIV.   *Presbyterian Assembly Buildings. The Assembly Hall.* See *150*.

PLATE XV. *The City Hall. The rotunda.* See *139.*

Haslemere, 46 Myrtlefield Park

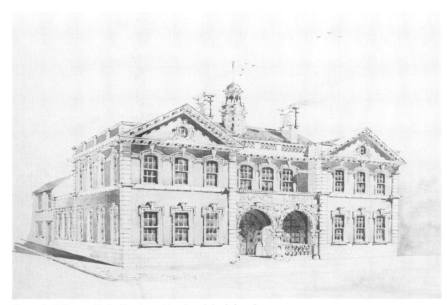

Carnegie Library, Falls Road: architect's original drawing

156 **HASLEMERE**, 46 Myrtlefield Park. **Frederick Tulloch**, 1905.

Tulloch built this Arts and Crafts suburban villa for himself and spared no effort to make it attractive. Some features of interest are the unusual chimney stacks, vertically striped in brick and roughcast; a small Tuscan order decorating the porch; and a set of colourful and pretty scenes in leaded lights across the ground floor windows.

157 **CARNEGIE LIBRARY**, Falls Road. **Watt and Tulloch**, 1905–8 (Courtney and Co., builders).

In 1905 out of a field of 30 entries limited to local architects Graeme Watt and Tulloch won the competition for three Carnegie Libraries in Belfast. Oldpark Road (1905–6) and Donegall Road (1907–9) are in a rather Tudoresque vein but the Falls Road branch is in that Edwardian form of English Classical style popularly known as 'Wrenaissance'. Spandrel angels carved by Rosamond Praeger. She also designed the female figure plaques of 'Literature' and 'Art' on the front door. These were originally bronze but have since been recast in fibreglass. Good scrolling art nouveau ironwork to stairway inside.

Carved work at Oldpark Library was by J.E. Winter.

158 **WHITLA MEDICAL INSTITUTE** (now closed), College Square North. **William J. Fennell**, 1902.

A neat little Tudoresque building in Scrabo stone with Dumfries dressings. Carved work by James Edgar Winter.

Close-by to the west on Durham Street is the Central T. B. Institute by Young and Mackenzie, 1916–18.

Fennell also designed two churches in Belfast: Cooke Centenary Presbyterian, Ormeau Road, 1890–2, and All Saints' Church of Ireland, University Street, 1898.

Carnegie Library, Falls Road: spandrel carving

Whitla Medical Institute in 1902

St Anne's Cathedral: the west end

159 ST ANNE'S CATHEDRAL
(Church of Ireland), Donegall Street.
Thomas Drew, 1898–1904 (H. Laverty & Sons, builders).

Worked on piecemeal until present day, with a succession of architects: Thomas Drew, 1896–1910; William Henry Lynn, 1910–15; Peter McGregor Chalmers of Glasgow, 1915–22; Richard Mills Close, 1922–4; Charles Nicholson of London, 1924–48; Thomas J. Rushton of London, 1948–63; John MacGeagh, 1963–79; Robert McKinstry, 1978–86.

In 1896 Drew proposed an ambitious design for a cathedral in English 13th century Gothic style, but on Lynn's advice he set it aside two years later for a Romanesque design which would be less expensive and more easily built in sections as funds became available. The building programme did indeed turn out to be very protracted and there were many departures from Drew's fine scheme. His wide and lofty nave was consecrated in 1904 but his elaborate proposal for deep gabled triple portals to the west front was much simplified and his proposal for a great belfry over the crossing was set aside, as was his design for the east end.

The west front, which in Drew's day had been left rough and unfinished, was eventually built to the designs of Charles Nicholson as a First World War Memorial, 1925–7. It has triple portals with groups of sculpture in the tympana, representing in the north door 'The Crucifixion', in the south door 'The Resurrection', and in the centre door 'Christ in Glory' surrounded by saints, some of them Irish, all carved by Esmond Burton. Upper portion of west gable itself also finished at this time, with label stops representing the four ruling passions of Industry, Strife, Love and Avarice carved by Burton. Bronze gates to west portals designed by Nicholson, made by Tudor Art Company of London, c.1929.

Inside, a scheme of carving of Drew's unfinished capitals and corbels was carried out between the wars although it had been initiated some years earlier. The ten capitals of the nave pillars are carved with the various occupations and pursuits of men; the four responds, to the east and west ends, represent the four cardinal virtues; over each of the capitals is a corbel carved with a great worthy of the Irish church, whilst at each corner of the nave are the four Archangels, Michael, Gabriel, Uriel and Raphael. The capitals of the pillars and responds represent from west to east on the north side, Courage, Science, Commerce, Healing, Agriculture, Music, and Justice. From east to west on the south side they represent Temperance, Theology, Shipbuilding, Masonry, Art, Women's Work, and Wisdom. They were mostly carved between 1925 and 1937 by the Ulster-domiciled Morris Harding from London, under the direction of Nicholson, but exceptions are Courage and Agriculture which were designed by Chalmers, and Justice which although designed by Nicholson was carved by Rosamond Praeger of Holywood, Co. Down. Stained glass in aisles and great west window carried out by James Powell & Sons, with the two rose windows of west end added by Archibald Nicholson, 1927.

Paving of aisles and part of nave with Irish marbles to designs of Charles Nicholson carried out 1929.

Semi-circular bapistry off west end of south aisle, in the position indicated for it by Drew, designed by Lynn, 1915, built 1922–4. Furnished and decorated 1927–8 to designs of Nicholson. His is the patterned floor of Portland stone and various Irish marbles; the font, a bowl of Portland stone inlaid with white alabaster and supported by columns of red marble on a black base; and the mosaic ceiling of 'The Creation' showing Fire, Air, Earth, and Water, executed with over 150,000 pieces of glass by Misses Gertrude and Margaret Martin. At the same time the Bath stone string courses were carved with children's heads by Rosamond Praeger. She was also responsible for the Carson memorial plaque in the south aisle.

Chapel of the Holy Spirit off west end of north aisle, domical ceilinged with a muniment room above, by Nicholson, 1930–2. Consecrated in 1932, coinciding with the fifteen hundredth anniversary of St Patrick's arrival at Saul, hence the St Patrick mosaic above the entrance arches.

Central crossing started in 1925 to design of Chalmers.

Eastern apse and ambulatory designed by Nicholson and Rushton, c.1947, completed 1959, but Rushton's proposal for a long eastern chapel and a great off-set eastern tower with a chapter house in the ground storey was not carried out.

South transept designed by MacGeagh, c.1968, completed 1974; and north transept, with its gigantic Celtic cross motif designed by MacGeagh, c.1964, completed 1981, but MacGeagh's designs for a tall thin spire over the crossing have not been built.
See pl. XVI.

Thomas Drew's original proposal for the west front

Thomas Drew's original proposal for the interior

St Anne's Cathedral: view from north-east

160 Former **SHARMAN D. NEILL PREMISES**, 36 Donegall Place.
Vincent Craig, 1903.

An idiosyncratic piece of commercial work by Craig in his favourite free manner with some remarkable details: a Baroque treatment of Free Renaissance, with the wavy lines of art nouveau. Built for the leading clockmaker in the city, hence the temporal theme of Winter & Thompson's carved freize. The original colour effect of red brick with light sandstone dressings now spoilt by being overpainted.

161 Former **CRYMBLE'S MUSIC SHOP**, 58 Wellington Place.
W. J. W. Roome, 1903.

A very pretty shop front, now a little spoiled, designed by an English architect who settled here in the nineties. Various classical elements combined in a sporty way and incorporating colourful vitreous mosaic spandrels with something of an art nouveau spirit.

Roome also designed the now demolished Athletic Stores on the other side of Wellington Place in 1896, where he had his office.

58 Wellington Place (from Crymble's Music Shop)

162 **MOUNTPOTTINGER Y.M.C.A.**, Albertbridge Road.
W. J. W. Roome, 1903 (McLaughlin & Harvey, builders).

The best display in Belfast of the recessed oriel, that window type so much enjoyed by the Queen Anne Revivalist followers of Norman Shaw. The big ventilator turret shown on William Roome's perspective sketch was not built.

The recessed oriel of 'Ipswich window' type was also used effectively by Roome at his Shankill Mission Building, Shankill Road, designed 1895 but upper storeys not finished until 1923 (now minus its large curved auditorium at the rear).

36 Donegall Place (former Sharman D. Neill premises)

Mountpottinger Y.M.C.A.: architect's perspective sketch

163 Former **SOMERSET'S LINEN FACTORY**, Hardcastle Street.
W. J. W. Roome, 1904 (J. & R. Thompson, builders).

The first reinforced concrete framed building in Ireland using the system of ferro-concrete construction devised by the Frenchman Francois Hennebique. Specialist ferro-concrete work carried out by the Yorkshire Hennebique Contracting Co. Ltd., directed by Louis-Gustave Mouchel. Seven storey extension by Blackwood and Jury, also using Hennebique system, 1911.

Other early reinforced concrete buildings in Belfast in the Hennebique system are the former Monarch Laundry, Donegall Road (where the single storey was intended to carry two more floors) by Jackson Smyth, 1906, and the Albion Works, Wellwood Street by Watt and Tulloch, 1909. A later Hennebique structure is the grandstand at Ravenhill Park Rugby Ground by Hobart and Heron, 1924.

Former Somerset's Linen Factory

164 Former **SCOTTISH TEMPERANCE BUILDINGS**,
(now Scottish Mutual), Donegall Square South.
Henry Seaver, 1904 (James Henry & Sons, builders).

Scottish stone from Dumfries and a few Scottish baronial features for a Scottish company's offices. A massive turreted and gabled block, actually more French chateau than Scottish castle in its general effect. The now plain parapets to the corner turrets formerly had battlements.

Nearby on Franklin Street is another building by Seaver, a six-storey warehouse designed for Sinclair & Co. in 1902 with a row of three three-storey oriels; building extended to Brunswick Street in 1906.

Former Scottish Temperance Buildings

165 **BAPTIST CHURCH**, Tennent Street.
James A. Hanna, 1904.

In the kind of late Gothic mode so popular in British non-conformist church work at the turn of the century. Good art nouveau floral patterns in glass, and curious flying mullions to the big gable window.

Hanna also designed the Baptist Churches on Antrim Road, 1896, and Clifton Park Avenue, 1904.

Tennent Street Baptist Church

Tennent Street Baptist Church: stained glass detail

166 **CO-OP BAKERY**, Ravenhill Avenue.
William J. Gilliland, 1904, with extensions in 1921 and 1929.

Octangular piers with ogee capstones, scalloped parapets, and white stone striped red brick: these are characteristic of Gilliland's late Queen Anne style. More modest examples of his work can be seen at the former Amalgamated Society of Woodworkers' Hall (now UCATT House), May Street, 1916, and a warehouse at the north-west corner of Queen Street, 1919.

Co-Op Bakery

Castle Buildings: detail

Castle Buildings: detail

167 **CASTLE BUILDINGS**, Castle Place.
Blackwood and Jury, 1904–5; extended 1907 (McLaughlin & Harvey, builders).

So called because it was erected on part of the site of the old 17th century Belfast Castle. Built as a large drapery emporium, of steel construction with a facing of 'Carrara-ware', a composite stone made by Doulton's of Lambeth. The most striking art nouveau facade in Ireland with well modelled freize and spandrel panels of swirling pomegranates and foliage, all designed by Percy Jury. Originally even more splendid than now, with traceried glazing bars to the windows and a wealth of ornamental fittings inside. Wrought iron balconies by William Greer.

Castle Buildings

168 **MAYFAIR BUILDING**, Arthur Square.
Blackwood and Jury, 1906 (Robert Corry, builder).

A big hulk of a building in stone banded brick with a dainty corner cupola, owing something to the example of Norman Shaw. The scrolled iron eaves brackets and art nouveau carved details are typical Percy Jury touches.

Mayfair Building

169 Former **LADIES' INDUSTRIAL SCHOOL**, Lancaster Street.
Blackwood and Jury, 1906–7 (McDowell, Leathem & Frazer, builders).

A quaint little building in red brick with dressings in cast concrete. A Diocletian window, a Palladian motif, and a 17th century English canopied doorway are all here in essence, but much modified, and treated in a very free manner. There is also some of Jury's pliant art nouveau-cum-classical ornament carved across the arch of the doorway.

Additions by R. S. Wilshere, 1932.

Ulster Bank, Albertbridge Road

Former Lancaster Street School

170 **ULSTER BANK**, Albertbridge Road.
Blackwood and Jury, 1908–10 (Thornbury Brothers, builders).

These architects built a number of Ulster Bank branches across the province in the first two decades of this century. Almost all are in some form of English classical style but usually very freely treated. This rather mannered Neo-Georgian branch at Mountpottinger presents an almost incoherent jumble of motifs in Mount Charles stone and Ruabon bricks. Arms carved by S. Hastings of Downpatrick.

The former Northern Bank nearby on the corner of Castlereagh Street and Albertbridge Road was by W. J. Gilliland, 1885, with porch added by S. P. Close, 1892.

Another surviving Ulster Bank in Belfast by Blackwood and Jury is the Newtownards Road branch, 1919, in a more austere classical manner.

171 **GOOD SHEPHERD CONVENT**, Ballynafeigh, Ormeau Road.
W. H. Byrne and Son of Dublin, 1906–11 (H. & J. Martin, builders). Chapel added 1913–17 (W. J. Campbell & Son, builders).

Extensive additions to a range of earlier nineteenth century buildings. Built of red brick and grey stone dressings in a typically institutional Gothic Revival style with much repetitive detailing. Fairly rich interior to the chapel with a predictable amount of elaborately carved stone, marble and decorative mosaic work.

Stretching behind these buildings is the large three storey red brick Penitentiary Building of the Catholic Refuge by Sherry and Hughes, 1868–9; gabled return to north, 1898, probably by J. J. McDonnell; and the original Convent House added to the south by Alex McAlister, 1884. McAlister's chapel of 1879 has now gone.

Sherry and Hughes' original gate lodge of 1868 altered and extended northwards to double its size by J. J. McDonnell, 1895.

Exactly opposite on Ormeau Road is another Gothic Revivalist Catholic complex, Nazareth House, first established here in 1876. The range of contiguous buildings begins at the south end with the two storey house, architect not known, and continues with the three storey extension to north by O'Neill and McCarthy, 1882, with a tower probably by J. J. McDonnell, 1900; tall chapel block by Mortimer Thompson, 1893–5; and Concert Hall and Dormitory by Hugh Lamont, 1934. Behind, fronting Ravenhill Road, is the Old Men's Home designed by J. J. McDonnell, 1923. Boundary wall, and presumably the little lodge tucked in alongside its gate, was by Alex McAlister, 1892.

Adjoining the Nazareth House site to north on Ormeau Road is Holy Rosary Roman Catholic Church designed by J. J. O'Shea, 1896–8 (H. & J. Martin, builders), in Scrabo sandstone with Dumfries dressings. Intended spire not built.

Good Shepherd Convent

Rathgar Street terrace

172 **CHICHESTER BUILDINGS**, Chichester Street.
Thomas J. Houston, 1906.

The first steel framed building in Belfast but very much altered. Originally a rather Elizabethan style gabled building to the upper floors but that has been completely changed. The ground floor, however, still survives as a rare example of an Edwardian shop front in Belfast with some quaint detailing around doorways by an architect who mostly built Arts and Crafts houses.

The other corner building of this block, at Calendar Street, is by Samuel Stevenson, 1894.

Chichester Buildings in its original state

173 **RATHGAR STREET**, off Lisburn Road.
Charles McAlister, 1907.

One of the most attractive Edwardian terraces in the city with its simple Queen Anne detailing and art nouveau leaded lights. Charles McAlister was also responsible for the quaint Old English style development further up Lisburn Road at Osborne with two blocks of shops facing a terrace, all with a half-timbered appearance contrived in cement, 1927.

Another good Edwardian terrace with Arts and Crafts detailing is 'Edenderry Terrace', Tennent Street, by Hill and Kennedy, 1907.

Cliftonville Moravian Church

A four storey gabled red brick tower-like building with some curiously old-fashioned detailing for the date, almost Gothick in effect, with wooden traceried windows and conoidal vaulting to carry an oriel over the doorway.

Sandy Row Orange Hall

174 CLIFTONVILLE MORAVIAN CHURCH, Oldpark Road.
James St John Phillips, 1908–9 (H. Laverty & Son, builders).

One of only five Moravian churches in Ireland. The intended tall spire was not built but what the church lacked in height as a result, it gained in quaint effect with its low overhung pyramidal roof to the tower. A nicely detailed church with flamboyant tracery and art nouveau leaded lights. The plan consists of a nave and chancel with only one aisle, but the possibility of another aisle was provided for in the curious way a nave arcade was built on the south side and then filled in, to be opened up easily if ever needed. The stained glass was by Ward and Partners, the fine chancel furniture in Austrian oak was made by Bell and Mayrs, and the wrought iron gates and railings by George Jones, all to the architect's designs.

The only other Moravian church in Belfast is at University Road, by Young and Mackenzie, 1884–7, in attractive but conventional Gothic style.

J. St J. Phillips also designed the small Methodist Church on Lisburn Road, 1906.

176 19 & 21 ALFRED STREET
James A. Hanna, 1911–12.

Hanna's warehouses are the most interesting of the Edwardian era and the years immediately following. Here at the former Walpole Brothers' linen warehouse is a facade of strong grid pattern with arches above and below, in red brick and Giffnock stone. Enlivened with freely treated Classical touches and vigorous zoomorphic carvings.

Also by Hanna are the drastically altered County Down Weaving Company's factory in Murray Street, 1908–10; factories in Bruce Street, 1906, and Howard Street South, 1905; and the former White, Tomkin's and Courage office block and Clarendon Mill in Corporation Street, with its doorway dated 1920.

19 & 21 Alfred Street

177 **LIGONIEL PUBLIC LIBRARY**, Ligoniel Road.
James G. Gamble, 1910.

Originally built as public washing baths this brick and Portland stone building in 'Wrenaissance' style was opened as a library in 1946. Designed by James G. Gamble, chief architect to Belfast Corporation. He would certainly have become familiar with English Classical detail during his ten years as clerk of works for Belfast City Hall.

Another building of the time, designed in the City Surveyor's Office under Horace Cutler, but probably Gamble's work, is the Gas Show Rooms, corner of Gresham and North Streets, 1908.

Ligoniel Public Library

178 **DALLAS**, 149 Malone Road.
C. F. A. Voysey of London, 1911–12.

A typical Voysey house, the only work in Ireland by one of the leading English Arts and Crafts architects at the turn of the century. Two storeys with an attic tucked under a massive steeply hipped roof of unbroken pitch but for a tower-like stairwell to the rear, all on a compact plan. The roughcast walls, sandstone dressings, Westmorland slates, iron casements, leaded lights, buttressed corners and big oak doors are all as one would expect in this neat example of Charles Voysey's 'abstract vernacular' style. Inside are some good brick arched fireplaces set in plain white walls, and a very fine open well stair with slatted balusters. Built for Robert Hetherington, a linen merchant.

Dallas, 149 Malone Road

179 **RIDDEL HALL**, 181a Stranmillis Road.
W. H. Lynn, 1913–15.

A large but rather dull manorial composition by the very elderly Lynn. (He died the year it was completed at the age of 86). Built of red brick made by the local Lagan Vale Works, and of Dumfries sandstone. No interiors of any interest but in the main corridor is a nice bronze memorial plaque to the Riddel Sisters by Rosamond Praeger showing young ladies reading books. The hall was originally built as a hostel for female students of Queen's University.

Riddel Hall

The Weir, 276 Malone Road

Ulster Bank, Cromac Street

180 THE WEIR, 276 Malone Road. **Blackwood and Jury**, 1916–17.

A large Old English style house built for the linen merchant Thomas Somerset. A conspicious sight overlooking the Lagan when approaching Shaw's Bridge from the east.

Other easily sighted domestic works by this firm are the large pair of Arts and Crafts style semi-detached houses at 1 & 3 Deramore Drive, 1902, and the much later Redhill (now Lakeside), Finaghy Road South, 1926.

181 ULSTER BANK, Cromac Street. **James A. Hanna**, 1919–22.

Like others who had indulged in quaint Arts and Crafts effects at the turn of the century Hanna later turned to a more dignified Classical manner as the new century wore on, at least for his buildings of a more public type. Here a corner cupola brings a touch of Baroque to an otherwise restrained design in stone-dressed red brick. Facing it is the even more restrained Northern Bank by Godfrey Ferguson, 1919.

182 BELFAST EAST POWER STATION, Wolff Road. **James G. Gamble**, 1919–23.

Situated on a peninsula of reclaimed land between the Victoria and the Musgrave Channels at the entrance to Belfast Harbour, this was originally known as The Harbour Power Station. It was renamed in 1958. Built of brick, with reinforced concrete by the Concrete Piling Co. and structural steelwork by Orr, Watt and Co. A very impressive sight, its big brick pilasters and Diocletian windows recalling the grandeur of ancient Rome. Extended 1925 and 1928.

The much more modern Belfast West Power Station across Victoria Channel was built to designs of Merz and McLellan, 1952–8.

Belfast East Power Station

183 **ULSTER MUSEUM**, Stranmillis Road.

James Cumming Wynnes of Edinburgh, designed 1914; built 1924–9 (H. & J. Martin, builders).

Of sixty-nine entries in the competition of 1913–14 for a Municipal Museum and Art Gallery the assessor John F. Burnet of Glasgow, the most celebrated Scottish architect of his time, adjudged a fellow Scot the winner. Burnet's own large French 'Beaux-Arts'-inspired Ionic colonnaded addition to the British Museum was near completion at the time and Wynnes clearly could not escape its influence. The winning design here was inevitably Neo-Classical too, but although academic, with an Ionic order derived from the Hellenic temple at Bassae, the outcome however is far from dull. The Portland stone masses are boldly treated in a vigorous way and given just a modicum of sculptured ornament. The main feature was to have been a long colonnade on the main front but this was never realised. The 1st World War delayed construction and in the end only one end portion of Wynnes' large scheme was completed, to slightly revised plans. Stone carving by Purdy & Millard, with sculptural work such as the prow of a galley at north end by James Edgar Winter. Iron work by R. J. McKinney. The building stood unfinished until the modern extension of 1963–71, for which see separate entry.

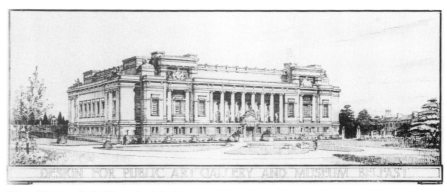

Ulster Museum: J.C. Wynnes' original intention for main front

Ulster Museum

184 **FIRST CHURCH OF CHRIST SCIENTIST**, University Avenue.

Clough Williams-Ellis of London, 1922–37.

A very attractive white walled Neo-Georgian group of church with school and caretaker's house, designed by a leading British architect. The whole complex was projected in 1922 but it took some years to achieve. The school was built first, by 1923, as a sort of pro-church, followed by the house in 1928. Finally the church was erected in 1936–7. A tall and striking composition, bedecked with urns and a Tuscan columned cupola, its well finished interior presents a fascinating mix of Art Deco and more traditional design. Unusual features are the star-like lights in the lobby, the painted starry ceiling in the uppermost room, and a pair of abstractly treated oak lecterns made by Purdy & Millard.

First Church of Christ Scientist: interior

First Church of Christ Scientist

185 Former **QUEEN'S UNIVERSITY AGRICULTURE BUILDING** (now Department of Geography), Elmwood Avenue.
R. Ingleby Smith, 1924–8.

A lively treatment of Neo-Georgian with Wrenian swags and a Mannerist doorway. Initially two storeyed on a rusticated basement and finished with a big cornice and parapet, its planned-for third storey was added in 1952 by Smith's successor as chief architect in the Ministry of Finance, T. F. O. Rippingham. Octagonal light wells to each wing with a fair-faced brick interior finish which was unusual at the time.

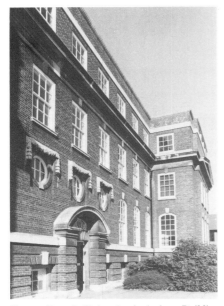

Former Queen's University Agriculture Building

186 **PUBLIC LIBRARY**, Shankill Road.
T. W. Henry, 1926–8 (Thornbury Brothers, builders).

A competition winning design by Tom Henry the architect brother of the famous Irish painter Paul Henry. The assessor was J. C. Wynnes of Edinburgh, architect of the Ulster Museum. Very restrained indeed with no extravagance in taste or cost; just a little curved Doric portico to add dignity to a public building.

Other works by Henry are the now spoiled Ulster Bank, and the handsome Ballysillan House (now a Convent), both on Crumlin Road and both designed 1919.

187 **STRANMILLIS COLLEGE**, Stranmillis Road.
R. Ingleby Smith, 1928–30 (H. & J. Martin, builders).

A very Frenchified Neo-Georgian block rather delicately detailed with a precious little tempietto on top. Of palatial layout on an axial plan. The unusual curved corners between the main block and wings accommodate the staircases and entrances. Beautifully built with walls of Cornish purple brick on a base of Portland stone, and a cornice and other dressings of the same stone.

Shankill Road Public Library

Stranmillis College

188 CHAPEL AT ST MARY'S DOMINICAN CONVENT,
Falls Road.
Padraic Gregory, 1926–30 (Felix G. O'Hare, builder).

A really fine chapel in a plain Gothic style. Spacious, austere, and delicate of line. It actually consists of two separate chapels, one for the community and the other adjoining it at the sanctuary, for boarders at the school. Rib vaulted ceilings in plaster and fan vaults to the overhanging gallery of the Nun's Choir. Fine oak fittings, especially the choir stalls in a simplified Gothic style. Mosaic floor in Celtic style to the sanctuary, laid by Oppenheimer & Co. of Manchester. Large decorative rose window by Messrs. Clarke of Dublin. Baldachino with Gothic open-work arches, built of Sienese and Pisan marbles, added by Gregory, 1935. Sanctuary windows by Gabriel Loire of Chartres, early 1960s.
See pl. XVII.

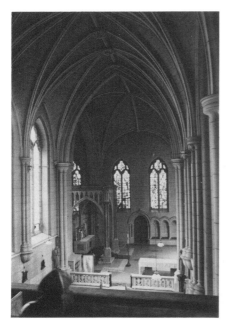

Chapel at St Mary's Dominican Convent

189 HEYN MEMORIAL HALL, Holywood Road.
R. H. Gibson, in association with Henry Seaver, 1928–9 (F. B. McKee & Co., builders).

One of the finest parish halls in the country it was built for St Mark's Church of Ireland, Dundela. Although Seaver was involved in the commission the design was surely the work of the younger man Robert Hanna Gibson. The big bay window in particular shows his declared admiration for Lutyens. In Tudor style with red brick walls, green Norwegian slates, wood panelled rooms, and timber mullioned windows. Some of the charm recently spoilt by the removal of some leaded casements.

Next door on Sydenham Avenue is the caretaker's house by Denis O'D. Hanna, 1956.

Bank of Ireland, Royal Avenue

Heyn Memorial Hall

190 **BANK OF IRELAND**, Royal Avenue.
J. V. Downes of McDonnell & Dixon of Dublin, 1928–30 (J. & R. Thompson, builders).

McDonnell and Dixon's first schemes for this site in 1924–6 were in a fairly predictable Baroque mode but a much more modern design by Joseph Downes was eventually built. Steel framed and clad in Portland stone it is a very striking building with a feature made of the large metal windows with metal panels between. Some Art Deco ornament on these panels and on the fine front entrance gates.

Downes was later to become a leading figure in the Modern Movement in the Republic of Ireland.

Woolworths

191 **ST CLEMENT'S CHURCH OF IRELAND**, Templemore Avenue.
Blackwood and Jury, 1928–30 (Courtney & Co., builders).

One of the last major works designed by P. M. Jury, in the Tudor Gothic style which he favoured for church work. Built of Buckley Junction bricks from England, with white stone dressings from Aughenheath in Scotland. Gargoyles of tower and other carved work was by S. & T. Hastings of Downpatrick; stained glass by W. J. Douglas and Sons.

Other inter-war churches to note are St Polycarp's Church of Ireland, Upper Lisburn Road, Finaghy, also by Blackwood and Jury, 1929–32; St Finian's Church of Ireland, Cregagh Park, 1930, and St Bartholomew's Church of Ireland, Stranmillis Road, 1930, both by W. D. R. Taggart; Cregagh Presbyterian, Cregagh Road, by James C. Stevenson, 1927; McCracken Memorial Presbyterian, Malone Road, by Hobart and Heron, 1932; and Lowe Memorial Presbyterian, Finaghy, by Tulloch and Fitzsimons, 1933–4. All show the dominance of traditional styles in ecclesiastical work of the time.

St Clement's Church of Ireland

193 **WOOLWORTHS**, High Street.
F. W. Woolworth & Co. Ltd. Construction Department of Liverpool, 1929.

The application of a kind of classical order and a stepped up parapet does not disguise the fact that this is a modern steel framed building underneath. Partly built for Montague Burton.

Not far away in Ann Street on the corner with Telfair Street, Burton's built more premises, a fairly standard stepped parapet arrangement but ornamented with elephant heads; designed by Harry Wilson of Leeds, 1931–2. Now changed hands it has lost its distinctive lettering but the jazzy detailing remains.

192 **BELFAST HOSPITAL FOR SICK CHILDREN**, Falls Road (in the grounds of the Royal Victoria Hospital).
Tulloch and Fitzsimons, 1928–32 (H. & J. Martin, builders).

Modified Georgian in style in rustic brick with the usual dressings of Portland stone. Very plain with only the main entrance bay being treated with any elaboration. Pleasant octagonal entrance hall, but the main interior interest lies in the coloured tile panels of nursery rhymes and other scenes on the walls of the Musgrave and Barbour wards, manufactured by Minton Hollins & Co. of Stoke-on-Trent to designs by Anne W. Yeames. Midway between this and the Royal Victoria Hospital itself is the Maternity Hospital, by Young and Mackenzie, 1932; a dull building but worth a look for the circular reliefs or tondi carved in the porch by Rosamond Praeger.

Belfast Hospital For Sick Children

84

194–198 **Schools designed by R. S. Wilshere**, Belfast Education Architect:

194 **STRANDTOWN SCHOOL**, North Road, 1928–30 (H. & J. Martin, builders).
195 **ELMGROVE SCHOOL**, Beersbridge Road, 1930–3 (J. & R. W. Taggart, builders).
196 **AVONIEL SCHOOL**, Avoniel Road, 1933–5 (W. Logan & Sons, builders).
197 **NETTLEFIELD SCHOOL**, Radnor Street, off Woodstock Road, 1934–6 (J. & R. W. Taggart, builders).
198 **BOTANIC SCHOOL**, Agincourt Avenue, 1936–9 (J. Moreland, builder).

Reginald Wilshere arrived here from Essex to become architect to Belfast Education Committee. Largely owing to his initiative, school design in Belfast was completely transformed. Between the wars he was to build a total of 26 schools in which air, light and sunshine were provided in abundance, and spaciousness and cheerfulness were to be the dominant characteristics. His schools vary in size and scale but all were well planned and laid out, superbly detailed and very well built. They were provided with such facilities as a single class-room for each class, a large assembly hall, and special rooms for instruction in science, cookery and art. Playgrounds were also provided although on occasion the roof had to be used for this if the site was very cramped. Efficient ventilation by natural means was achieved by cross-ventilation and by open-air corridors, and great care was taken with lighting arrangements. Indeed, these were the first modern schools to be built anywhere in Ireland.

As regards appearance they range from the Neo-Georgian to the outright modernistic. Traditional references abound but there are also hints of modern German, Scandinavian and Dutch work. Parallels with Dudok in particular continually come to mind. Most are built in brick with dressings of artificial stone, and roofs covered with Roman tiles, whilst classrooms were frequently finished in varying shades of colour. At many of them there is an associated caretaker's house, each one in itself a gem. A tour round these schools is a real delight; as an inter-war series they must surely have an important place in a wider than local context.

Some features of interest to note are the rather Swedish looking water tower with a teak lantern at **Nettlefield**, and Wilshere's first use of all-glass elevations at the same school; the very Danish looking stepped gable at **Elmgrove**; the sculpted panel showing 'Education reclining below the Tree of Knowledge' by George McCann over the main entrance, and the little wrought-iron elephant window grilles by Musgrave & Co., next to the cloakrooms at **Avoniel**; the roof top terrace, and the now spoilt amphitheatre-like outdoor seated courtyard at **Botanic**; and finally the subtle use of lighter brick for dressings in the otherwise dark toned rustic brick of **Strandtown School**, a building that was awarded the RIBA Ulster Architecture Medal for 1930.

Strandtown School

Elmgrove School

Avoniel School

Avoniel School: window grille

Nettlefield School

Other Wilshere schools worth noting are (with the dates the designs were prepared): *Mountcollyer*, Limestone Road, 1927; *Riga Street School*, 1928; *Linfield*, Blythe Street, 1929; *Kelvin*, Roden Street, 1931; *Argyle*, 1933, and *Charters Memorial*, 1939, both North Howard Street; *Edenbrooke*, Tennent Street, 1934; *McQuiston Memorial* (now School of Music), Donegall Pass, 1934; *The Model*, Cliftonville Road, 1936; *Grove*, North Queen Street, 1937; *Carrs Glen*, Oldpark Road, 1938; and *Orangefield*, Marina Park, 1938.

Botanic School

The Royal Courts of Justice

199 THE ROYAL COURTS OF JUSTICE, Chichester Street.
James G. West of London, 1928–33 (Stewart & Partners, builders).

Along with Parliament Buildings this was one of the two big monuments of the newly established state of Northern Ireland. A rather weighty looking classical building of steel-framed structure faced with Portland stone, with a giant Corinthian order and lots of Gibbsian detail. Recessed porticoes to both the Chichester Street and May Street frontages lead to large vestibules giving access to a large and impressive hall, 140 feet long and panelled in Travertine marble.

The Welsh born West was a senior architect in the Imperial Office of Works, Westminster; he was knighted in 1936. *See* pl. XIX.

200 ST CHRISTOPHER'S CHURCH OF IRELAND, Mersey Street.
R. H. Gibson, in association with Henry Seaver, 1931.

The pantiled roof and rustic brick suggest the hand of Gibson here although Seaver signed the drawings. A very crisp and neat treatment of Romanesque although the porch is a little mean.

A less pleasantly coloured and textured church of fairly similar style was built by Seaver at St Martin's, Kenilworth Street, 1933, originally hemmed in by houses but now standing alone where the Newtownards Road begins.

St Christopher's Church of Ireland

PLATE XVI. *St Anne's Cathedral. The baptistry. See 159.*

PLATE XVII. *St Mary's Dominican Convent Chapel. Interior.* See *188.*

201 BRADBURY BUILDINGS, Bradbury Place.
J. D. Gordon, 1932.

A charming little brick range built as shops, offices and living quarters. Its quiet Neo-Georgian symmetry is offset by a jaunty pavilion overlooking the railway line, pagoda-like with a copper galleon finial.

Bradbury Buildings

202 THE HARTY ROOM, QUEEN'S UNIVERSITY DEPARTMENT OF MUSIC, University Road.
W. Forsyth of London, 1932–3 (W. Dowling, builder).

Originally built as a new dining hall for the Students' Union of Queen's University, this neat little Tudor Gothic building has one of the finest hammer-beam roofs in Ireland. No iron bolts or screws were used in the construction, the whole having been put together with oak pins. Rather church-like with a 'transept' to each side, each one marked by two arches through which run very large oak beams. Outside are multi-coloured rustic Ulster bricks laid with broad joints, dressings of Weldon stone from Northamptonshire, Westmorland green slates, and cast lead rainwater heads. Clearly a gem of a building in its own right it nevertheless still sits oddly with the earlier building to which it is joined, the former Students' Union in harsh red brick, by Robert Cochrane of the Board of Works in Dublin, 1896, extended to the south by W. H. Lynn, 1911. Forsyth was much involved with educational buildings in England having designed Hull University College and worked at Eton and Harrow. He was also consulting architect to the National Trust.

The Harty Room, Queen's University Music Department

203 OUR LADY'S HOSPITAL, Beechmount, Falls Road.
Frank McArdle, 1932–5 (J. J. Doyle, builder).

Situated on a slope above Falls Road and reached by a long avenue; a neat little Gothic design in that combination of bright red brick and light stone dressings so frequently used by traditionalist architects in the inter-war years. A symmetrical E-plan two storey building, with a small chapel built alongside, 1934–5. Both lie behind the convent which is located in Beechmount, a plain early 19th century house with Doric *in antis* portico, for long the home of the Riddel family.

Other works by McArdle are St Mary's Secondary School, Barrack Street, 1925–6; the Chapel at Poor Clares Convent, Cliftonville Road, 1928–32; Holy Cross Convent, Glen Road, 1934; the Nurses Home at the Mater Hospital, Crumlin Road, 1931–4; and the much later and more modern Roman Catholic Church of Our Lady of Perpetual Succour, Deanby Gardens. designed 1954.

Our Lady's Hospital

Telephone House, photographed in 1935

204 **TELEPHONE HOUSE** (Central Telephone Exchange), Cromac Street. **T. F. O. Rippingham** under R. I. Smith. 1932–4 (Stewart & Partners, builders).

A very massive steel-framed block, modernist yet in a Neo-Georgian mould. Originally intended to have had walls of Mourne granite, but due to expense that stone was confined to a band at sixth floor level and to the base, with Ruabon bricks of silver grey tone used for most of the walling, and bands of Portland stone at the top. The elevations have an Art Deco cum classical look with windows deep set in tall vertical strips. Note the zig-zag pattern on the cast aluminium panels: a modern motif for a modern building housing a modern commodity. Royal coat of arms above door carved by Morris Harding.

Initially laid out as an L-shaped building it was later extended in the same style in 1959 to form a squarish block, with a pitched roof of handmade Spanish tiles over a new seventh storey added around the whole block.

A series of plain Neo-Georgian satellite exchanges was built at various points in the city, also under the direction of R. Ingleby Smith. Examples are to be found at Paulett Avenue and at Windsor Park, 1933 (raised a storey in 1966).

205 **GRAIN SILOS OF THE 1930s AT BELFAST HARBOUR.**

The silo is an unusual type of building with windows only on top and bottom floors, the central space containing the great reinforced concrete storage bins. The first of these great structures here was at **Pacific Flour Mills**, Northern Road, built for Joseph Rank Ltd. to the designs of Gelder & Kitchen of Hull, 1931–3 (Courtney & Co., builders). Part of

Grain Silos at Belfast Harbour. Left to right: Barnett's Silo, Hall's Silo, Pacific Flour Mills

the original mill and warehouse fronting Pollock Dock have now been demolished but the main silo still stands along with those added in 1936 and 1939. Built of reinforced concrete, the details supplied by L. G. Mouchel & Partners of Westminster, the walls faced in red Laganvale brick with dressings of Snowcrete.

To the south across Pollock Dock is **Hall's Silo**, Dufferin Road, by Henry Simon of Stockport, 1936–7. Built in the Hennebique system, the Consulting Engineers being Mouchel & Partners.

To the north-east along Dufferin Road is **Barnett's Silo** by R. Duncan, 1936–7 (McLaughlin & Harvey, builders). The Consulting Engineer here was William Littlejohn Philip of Corsham, Wiltshire, a renowned specialist in this type of reinforced concrete structure.

206 ST JUDE'S PARISH HALL, Ravenhill Road.

R. H. Gibson, 1933–4 (William Dowling, builder).

A very pleasantly textured building in rustic brick with a pantiled roof. Vaguely Lombardic in style with a Neo-Georgian touch but that style gives way in the interior to a muted Art Deco in the big hall upstairs. Doorway later brought out from gable to form a front porch, by Gibson, 1940.

Awarded the RIBA Ulster Architecture Medal in 1938.

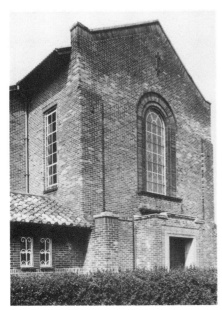

St Jude's Parish Hall

207 THE KING'S HALL, Lisburn Road, Balmoral.

A. Leitch and Partners of London and Glasgow, 1933–4 (J. & R. Thompson, builders).

This prominent landmark on the Lisburn Road is the exhibition hall and headquarters of the Royal Ulster Agricultural Society. A powerful piece of engineers' architecture, with a few Art Deco details being the only concession to ornamentation. A wide-span

The King's Hall

The King's Hall: the foyer

space that was shown off to very great effect until the step-form roof was recently covered over. Essentially a skeleton of arches and stiffening panels built entirely of ferro-concrete using the Considere system.

Elsewhere in the grounds the Hennebique system of ferro-concrete was used in the Sale Ring and the Grandstand designed by T. W. Henry, 1920, and in another grandstand further to the east, by Leitch and Partners, 1931.

90

208 736 ANTRIM ROAD
Hugh Gault, 1934.

Hugh Gault designed three flat-roofed modernist houses in Belfast: in Lismoyne Park, 1933; Cleaver Gardens, 1937; and here on a site below Cave Hill. The roof top terrace takes advantage here of a panoramic view over Belfast Lough. Surrounded by more traditional types this house still stands out as a breakaway from convention. Behind it in Glencoe Park is a less striking example by William Porte, 1935.

Amongst others to be found around the suburbs are a group on Old Holywood Road, by John MacGeagh, 1935, and one at Belmont Drive, by Anthony Lucy, 1937.

736 Antrim Road

209 IMPERIAL HOUSE, Donegall Square East.
Kendrick Edwards, 1935 (Thomas McKee & Sons, builders).

A framed office building with a large expanse of white matt-finished terracotta tiles covering most of the facade, and greenish granite below. Described at the time as 'modern without being freakish and traditional without being imitative', although the classical touches are obvious.

Edwards also designed Donegall Chambers on the corner of Donegall Place and Fountain Lane in 1932, with towered front and set-back upper storeys.

Former Sinclair's Store

210 Former SINCLAIR'S STORE, Royal Avenue.
James Scott, 1935.

A jazzy step-form gabled frontispiece in a creamy coloured faience added by Scott in 1935 to his earlier more classically tricked out Sinclair's Department Store of 1926 which runs between Royal Avenue and North Street.

Scott was also architect for the fine red brick linen warehouse with a good classical doorway in stone on the corner of Linen Hall Street and Franklin Street, designed for Samuel Lamont & Sons in 1923; demolished in 1987.

Imperial House

211 CURZON CINEMA, Ormeau Road.
James McB. Neill, 1935–6.

One of the most characteristic building types of the thirties, usually with very *moderne* detailing, was the cinema. The type has not fared well in Belfast and some of the best work has disappeared. Although at best only a moderate example the Curzon is one of the few that has not closed, and although much altered it still looks tolerably like a work of the thirties. Originally, it had a glazed central tower breaking the skyline, laid over a lower glazed parapet, but all that glazing in 'Lenscrete' has now gone and the tower has been reduced to a fin.

Neill was the local cinema specialist. Other examples by him still standing in Belfast are The Strand, Holywood Road, 1935; the former Troxy (later Grove Theatre), Shore Road, 1936; and the former Majestic (now a warehouse), Lisburn Road, 1935–6.

Also still standing in Belfast, although no longer functioning, are a few thirties cinemas by other local architects: former Ambassador (now shop), Cregagh Road, by John MacGeagh, 1936; former Park (now closed), Oldpark Road, by Thomas Eager, 1936; and former Stadium (now a leisure centre), Shankill Road, by Robert Sharpe Hill, 1936. The former Ritz (now A.B.C.), Fisherwick Place was by Kemp and Tasker of London, 1935.

Curzon Cinema

212 B.B.C. HEADQUARTERS,
Ormeau Avenue.
James Miller of Glasgow, 1936–9.

A steel frame with reinforced conrete floors and roof, and a facing of sand faced bricks on an artificial stone base. An uninspired building. Like so many others of this era it has Neo-Georgian overtones.

B.B.C. Headquarters

213 ST ANTHONY'S ROMAN CATHOLIC CHURCH,
Woodstock Road.
Padraic Gregory, 1936–8 (P. & F. McDonnell, builders).

A very fine Neo-Gothic church by a very talented poet-architect who clearly could recapture the spirit of the past yet still spice it with a novel touch. Note the clever way a Latin cross is created in the gable tracery. Built of Ballycullen stone from Scrabo, with dressings of pre-cast stone. Stained glass by Earley & Co. of Dublin.

The small church hall to the west was by S. J. McAvoy, 1931.

Other church works by Gregory are the apse with chancel furnishings and mosaic decorations added to St Columcille's, Upper Newtownards Road, 1927–9; the fine balachino and other marble work, and mortuary chapel, added to St Paul's, Falls Road, 1939; and St Therese de L'Enfant Jesus, Somerton Road, 1936–9, with its rose window designed to represent the petals of a flower (J. & R. Thompson, builders).

St Anthony's Roman Catholic Church

Smyth Halls

216 NORTH STREET ARCADE, between North Street and Donegall Street. **Cowser & Smyth**, 1936 (F. B. McKee & Co. Ltd., builders).

A thirties shopping arcade, not too jazzy in appearance but *moderne* all the same. Above the Donegall Street entrance is a figured panel saved from the old Brookfield Linen Company warehouse (by W. H. Lynn, 1869 and 1881) which was demolished to make way for this arcade.

North Street Arcade

214 **SMYTH HALLS**, Lisburn Road. **John MacGeagh**, 1930–3 (C. & W. McQuoid, builders).

From the Tudor Revivalist style used at his Ballymacarrett Presbyterian Church Hall in 1927, MacGeagh turned here to the Neo-Georgian mode with which he is more usually associated. Faced with rustic brick from Co. Tyrone, carefully graded with variations in tone. Some restrained Art Deco patterns in the wrought iron gates and grilles worked by Musgrave & Co.

Next door is the former manse by James Mackinnon, 1880.

215 **GOSPEL HALL**, Albertbridge Road. **John MacGeagh**, 1935–6 (James Buckley & Sons, builders).

The 'Belfast Tabernacle and Bible School' as it was originally known follows the usual MacGeagh pattern for this type of building, with a big hall flanked by smaller blocks although more variegated in form than usual. Neo-Georgian-cum-Romanesquoid in its round arched work with a Mediterranean feel to its pantiled roof.

Masonic Hall, Crumlin Road

Gospel Hall, Albertbridge Road

217 **MASONIC HALL**, Crumlin Road. **John MacGeagh**, 1938–40 (C. & W. McQuoid, builders).

Steel-framed with a facing of brick and dressings of artificial stone. An extremely plain design with two shops incorporated in the frontage. Twin pillars carry a deep over-door of simple Art Deco design with a figured panel by Morris Harding, 1939.

218 **THE SIR WILLIAM WHITLA
HALL**, Queen's University of Belfast,
University Road.
John MacGeagh, with Edward Maufe of
London, consulting architect.
Designed 1937, begun 1938–9, finished
1945–9 (F. B. McKee & Co. Ltd., builders).

Almost complete when war broke out caus-
ing work to be suspended for almost seven
years, John MacGeagh's masterpiece was
not opened until after the war. It won for
him and his consultant Maufe the RIBA
Ulster Architecture Medal for 1950. Of
handmade rough-surfaced facing bricks
with Chipsham and York stone dressings, its
blocky form sits serenely overlooking the
front lawn of Queen's University. Stone
carvings designed by Gilbert Bayes of London; executed by Morris Harding. Over
main entrance is the University coat of arms
above a globe with figures of Aesculapius,
the god of medicine, and a Scribe, depicting
Sir William Whitla's services to healing and
to learning. On the west side, the keystones
depict the faculties of the University, and on
the east side, the trade and commerce of
Ulster. On the west wall is a bronze bust of
the benefactor, the work of Bayes, set in a
niche with a surround carved by Harding.

This building is not to be confused with
the less interesting Whitla Memorial Hall by
Alan H. Hope of Dublin, opened in 1935, in
the grounds of Methodist College nearby.

219 **HENRY GARRETT BUILDING**,
Stranmillis College, Stranmillis Road.
T. F. O. Rippingham (Chief Architect,
Ministry of Finance), 1944.

Functionalist ideals and traditional values
are welded together in this nicely balanced
building. A graceful note is struck in the
entrance elevation with the double height
porch set in a slightly bowed wall. Elsewhere
blocky forms are played off against long
horizontal lines. The circular window in a
concrete surround was a favourite motif of
Rippingham.

The Sir William Whitla Hall: west side

The Sir William Whitla Hall: entrance hall

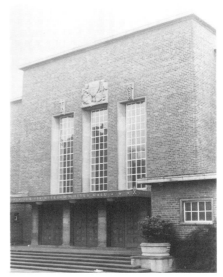

The Sir William Whitla Hall: entrance front

The Henry Garrett Building

220 **CREGAGH HOUSING ESTATE**, Cregagh Road and Mount Merrion Avenue, Cregagh.
T. F. O. Rippingham for the Northern Ireland Housing Trust, 1945–50.

One of the earliest and most admired schemes by the Housing Trust, Cregagh was notable in having continuous frontages with no views of back gardens. There is plenty of light and space here in this varied layout of terraces, closes and small squares, with a total of 924 dwellings on a 91 acre site. Owing to the scarcity of materials at the time a strictly utilitarian type of design and structure was necessary. Lack of roofing tiles or slates and a shortage of bricklayers led to the adoption of flat concrete roofs and confined brickwork to the outer walls only. Shops and community buildings were built to flank the approaches, at the main entrance off Cregagh Road.

In the central open space is **Cregagh Primary School**, built in 1949 to a novel and original design by Rippingham, with classrooms separated and staggered along two sides of a playground. The Assembly Hall and Dining Hall close each end. Very modern in treatment with light and airy interiors.

221 **QUEEN'S UNIVERSITY GEO-LOGY BUILDING**, Elmwood Avenue.
John MacGeagh, with E. Maufe of London, consulting architect, 1949–54.

The only part built of a great Beaux Arts inspired plan for the Elmwood Avenue to Fitzwilliam Street area. An interesting modern treatment of Neo-Georgian with metal framed windows set very flush to the walls. Urns were intended to go on the corner pedestals and a sculpted figure to stand in the central niche where only unworked blocks are now to be seen.

Cregagh Housing Estate

Cregagh Estate: the Primary School

Queen's University Geology Building

Masonic Hall, Rosemary Street

222 **MASONIC HALL**, Rosemary Street.
Young and Mackenzie, 1950 (Stewart & Partners, builders).

The area around Rosemary Street and Bridge Street was badly blitzed in the 1941 air raids. Young and Mackenzie did much of the rebuilding. At the Masonic Hall they stuck to tradition with a classical frontage in stone, with timber sash tripartite windows and a large triangular pediment.

Around the corner in Bridge Street the same architects moved from the Neo-Georgian style of the former Arnott's Building on the east side, 1955, to a post-'Festival of Britain' modern style for the block on the west side, 1957.

110 Malone Road

223 110 MALONE ROAD
Henry Lynch-Robinson, 1949.

The first modernist houses of the 1930s in Ulster were quite tied to tradition in terms of plan and arrangment, despite their new looks. A decade or so later a few more original types were attempted. This Belfast example was quite celebrated in its time. It was built only after a successful appeal to the Minister of Health and Housing against the Corporation Building Inspector's refusal of permission to build. Low mono-pitch roof with a cantilevered reinforced concrete stair inside. The original metal glazing bars have now been taken out.

224 DAVID KEIR BUILDING, Stranmillis Road.
Lanchester and Lodge of London, 1951–7.

A monumental science block for Queen's University, steel-framed, essentially modern and utilitarian in purpose, yet styled in Neo-Georgian brick and Portland stone. Axially planned, it spreads between two diverging roads with long corridors and sterile courtyards. Shades of Giles Gilbert Scott at Cambridge and Herbert Rowse at Liverpool in the choice of towered forms that offset the long sweeping, rather *moderne*, horizontal lines of the Stranmillis Road frontage.

225 CONGREGATIONAL CHURCH, Donegall Street.
Rebuilt by **Samuel Stevenson and Sons**, 1952.

A Gothic-Revivalist street frontage of various dates by various hands, although nothing can now be seen of the church that Raffles Brown of Dublin built here in 1859–60, set back a bit from the street. Later in 1871 street-front additions were made to each side by L. Macassey with shops on the ground floor, classrooms above, and a grand arrangement of steps in the middle. Some of this went when the church front was brought forward by John Seeds in his reconstruction of 1932–4 after a fire, with the tracery and the shop fronts given a Perpendicular treatment. Finally, after wartime damage, the upper part of the front facade was reconstructed in 1952, with a concentric circled rose window as its main motif.

Donegall Street Congregational Church, before the fire of 1932

The David Keir Building

Donegall Street Congregational Church

226 **ST PATRICK'S SECONDARY SCHOOL**, Antrim Road.
McLean & Forte, 1952–5 (Orlit (N.I.) Ltd., builders).

A strange looking affair, on an unconventional plan. Built in the Orlit system of precast concrete blocks which had already been used for some housing estates a few years before. In the school grounds are two houses worth noting: Tieve Tara on Somerton Road, by Watt and Tulloch, 1907; and Barnageeha, completely surrounded by the school, for which see separate entry. McLean & Forte were also responsible for St Patrick's Primary School, North Queen Street, 1953–5.

227 **GREENWOOD SCHOOL**, Upper Newtownards Road.
Lynch-Robinson and McKinstry, 1954–7.

A straightforwardly modern building for the mid-fifties in mostly modern materials with more colour than usual introduced in the panels. Pre-cast concrete slabs to assembly hall gable, and curtain wall glazing along the classrooms. There is a little fussiness in the window pattern and a cranky line to the ironwork but that is expected in post-'Festival of Britain' design.

228 **METHODIST CHURCH**, Cavehill Road.
Young and Mackenzie, 1953.

A dumpy towered symmetrical composition in brick with swept roofs, designed in that indeterminate style that was common just after the war, in which old and new were blended together. Probably of modern Dutch or Scandinavian inspiration.

Other churches by Young and Mackenzie of this period are the Methodist Church, Newtownards Road, 1949; Rosemary Presbyterian, North Circular Road, 1950; and Newington Presbyterian, Limestone Road, 1951–2.

St Patrick's Secondary School

Greenwood School

Methodist Church, Cavehill

St Barnabas' Church of Ireland

229 **ST BARNABAS' CHURCH OF IRELAND**, Duncairn Gardens.
John MacGeagh, 1955–6 (F. B. McKee & Co., builders).

A kind of Swedish purity pervades this Neo-Gothic work, built to replace an earlier church on the site destroyed in the blitz. Traditional in form but modern in treatment it shows MacGeagh's admiration for Edward Maufe's work at Guildford Cathedral in Surrey.

In similar modern Neo-Gothic is MacGeagh's St Silas' Church of Ireland, Cliftonville Road, 1956–8, also built to replace a church lost in the blitz.

Orangefield Presbyterian Church

Transport House

230 **ORANGEFIELD PRESBYTERIAN CHURCH**, Castlereagh Road.
Gordon McKnight, 1955–7 (Sloan Brothers, builders).

The earlier gabled church hall by J. F. Hay of 1938 probably gave the cue for the general shape of the post-war church alongside, but McKnight's treatment of detail is clearly 'Festival of Britain' inspired. The attenuated porch and the finialed belfry tower are entirely of their period.

To the west on the other side of Castlereagh Road is St John Evangelist Church of Ireland, exactly contemporary but in a much more traditional vein, Neo-Gothic in style, by Gibson and Taylor, 1955–7.

231 **TRANSPORT HOUSE**, High Street.
J. J. Brennan, 1956–9 (P. Carvill & Sons, builders).

A dramatic working of International Style themes but sombre and heavy in feel. Entirely clad in tilework, mostly green, with curved end wall sailing out on black pilotis or pillars. Built for the Amalgamated Transport and General Workers' Union.

Brennan's offices for the Amalgamated Engineering Union, Antrim Road, designed in 1964 are just as distinctive though less dramatically arranged.

232 **CHURCH OF THE PENTECOST**, (Church of Ireland), Mount Merrion Avenue, Cregagh.
Denis O'D. Hanna, 1961-3.

Built by an architect concerned with the blending of traditional and modern styles and also with fostering of modern ecclesiastical art. To an earlier hall of 1956 Hanna added this gabled red brick church with steeply pitched roof on concrete portal frames. Aluminium dove of the Pentecost above the Holy Table, by Elizabeth Campbell; Wheat and tares decorating the window in aluminium and brass, by Desmond Kinney; and stone plaques in the garden wall by David Pettigrew.

Church of the Pentecost

The Synagogue: interior detail

The Synagogue

233 **THE SYNAGOGUE**, Somerton Road.
Yorke, Rosenberg and Mardall of London, 1961–4 (McLaughlin & Harvey, builders).

Designed by Eugene Rosenberg this is one of the most accomplished modern buildings in Belfast. A fine lofty circular hall of worship in brick with a 'Star of David' configuration to the concrete beams inside, carrying a folded timber roof, all handled with great assurance. Interior very smartly finished. The candelabrum, the incised lettering in the Portland stone wall of the ark, and the formalised Hebrew letters fixed to the sliding bronze doors of the ark, are all by the Israeli sculptor Nehemia Azaz.

Minor Synagogue and Community House to the right, by W. H. McAlister and Partners, 1966.

234 **Queen's University MICROBIO-LOGY BUILDING**, Royal Victoria Hospital, Grosvenor Road.
Casson and Condor of London, 1961–5.

Surely one of the high points in modern architecture in Belfast. It seems to recall the 'heroic period' of the Modern Movement in its uncompromising boldness, sleek form and functionalist stance. Designed by the distinguished English architect Sir Hugh Casson with his partner Neville Condor.

Microbiology Building, Royal Victoria Hospital

235 **ST BERNADETTE'S ROMAN CATHOLIC CHURCH**, Rosetta Road.
P. & B. Gregory, 1966.

A thoroughly modern design in reinforced concrete and brickwork designed by Brian Gregory. A large and open interior on a fan-shaped plan. Bronze figure of Christ, in the sanctuary, by Elizabeth Frink.
See pl. XX.

St Bernadette's Roman Catholic Church

St Clement's Retreat Chapel

St Clement's Retreat Chapel: interior

Ulster Museum Extension

236 ST CLEMENT'S RETREAT CHAPEL, Antrim Road.
Corr and McCormick of Londonderry, 1966–7.

By the leading post-war church architects in Ireland Frank Corr and Liam McCormick. A thoroughly modern piece of ecclesiastical architecture, crisply built in brick and with a shallow copper sheathed timber shell dome. *Vesica piscis*-like in plan but with its ends indented and glazed. Abstract patterned stained glass by Helen Moloney.

The Retreat House, in two wings, to each side of the chapel, was designed by J. J. Brennan, 1959–60. He also designed the earlier small monastery on the hillside below, in 1961, and St Gerard's Redemptorists' Roman Catholic Church at the bottom of the site, on Antrim Road, in 1953.

237 ULSTER MUSEUM EXTENSION, Botanic Gardens, Stranmillis Road.
Francis Pym of London, 1963–71 (McLaughlin & Harvey, builders).

A boldly sculptural conception in concrete, the result of a competition in 1963 for a large extension to the earlier Neo-Classical building by J. C. Wynnes, left unfinished in 1929. The new work which started in 1966 is cleverly spliced onto the old by drawing out the channelled rustications and other mouldings of the earlier building until they butt against the new blocky forms that seem to jut out at random. Carried out in concrete left untouched after the shuttering was removed. All a bit heavy and sombre outside with mixed results inside. There were 83 entries in the competition which was assessed by Sir Leslie Martin of Cambridge.

St Patrick's Church of Ireland, Jordanstown

Part Two

THE ENVIRONS

Arranged chronologically within three areas:
North   South   East

N1 THE WHITE HOUSE (now a Gospel Hall), Whitehouse Park, Whitehouse.
Early 1600s.

An example of early 17th century domestic architecture; a rectangular thick stone walled house with defensive circular towers, or flankers as they are known, at the front corners and a central curved projection to the rear probably for stairs. Although only one storey in height now, it could well have had as many as four or five, originally. It was no doubt gabled, with conical caps to the flankers, like other fortified plantation houses or castles. The brick archways were inserted during repair work in the early nineteenth century. Often known as 'King William's House': it was at this point on the lough that William III's army landed in 1690, and tradition has it that the King stayed in this house on the night of 14th June that year.

N2 ST PATRICK'S CHURCH OF IRELAND, Jordanstown Road, Jordanstown.
Lanyon, Lynn, and Lanyon, 1865–8 (James Henry, builder).

Inspired by the 12th century conjoined round tower and church of St Finghin at Clonmacnoise, W. H. Lynn created here at Jordanstown one of the prettiest Celtic Revivalist churches in Ireland. Hiberno-Romanesque in general intention, but with an un-Irish curved apse, and a typical High Victorian polychrome treatment of masonry with white Scrabo sandstone walls banded in red. Interior walls lined with pink and black brick. Derbyshire marble reredos and Caen stone arcades added to the sanctuary in 1894. Good stained glass windows in the chancel, depicting four great Irish saints – Patrick, Comgall, Brigid and Columba – with Celtic ornamental borders, by Clayton & Bell of London, 1868. The three windows in the south aisle were by Cox & Buckley of London and Youghal, 1891. Typanum in porch of the slave-boy Patrick kneeling in prayer on the hill of Slemish, carved by Rosamond Praeger, 1933.

The White House

St Patrick's Church, Jordanstown: 'St Patrick' stained glass window

N3 **ST MARY'S STAR OF THE SEA ROMAN CATHOLIC CHURCH**, Whitehouse.
John O'Neill, 1865–7 (John Ross, builder).

A striking Gothic Revival church in Early English style built of black basalt with light sandstone dressings. High roofed, with the nave and chancel at the same height, and a very tall tower and spire which was not actually erected until 1899. The original ornamental painted stencil-work to the chancel walls has long been obliterated and O'Neill's elaborate pulpit more recently removed , but the impressive High Victorian altar and reredos by Thomas Earp of London still remains. Built of Caen stone with red marble inlays and colonnettes it has four saints in niches to each side of a much-crocketed canopy over a crucified Christ.

Throne Hospital

N4 **THRONE HOSPITAL**, Whitewell Road.
Timothy Hevey, 1874.

A vigorous and original treatment of French Gothic in polychrome brick with white Scrabo dressings. This characteristic piece of High Victorian design was originally built as a Children's Hospital by John Martin of Shrigley, Co. Down in memory of his son Samuel. The much altered entrance block and Convalescent Home to the left was added by Thomas Jackson and Son, 1877 (H. & J. Martin, builders).

N5 **THE BLEACH GREEN VIADUCT**, to north of Glenville Road, Whiteabbey.
W. K. Wallace CE, 1931–3.

This was the largest ferro-concrete viaduct in the British Isles in its time. Built to carry the main double-track railway line from Belfast to Londonderry across Valentine's Glen, it combined with the smaller viaduct which passes under it to form the only flying junction in Northern Ireland. Of very modern design, the large curved main-line viaduct has three main parabolic arches between large piers; the straight down-shore viaduct has just one main parabolic arch flanked by smaller arches. The whole of the reinforced concrete work was carried out by the railway company by direct labour, the men being taken from local labour exchanges. R. L. McIlmoyle CE, of the LMS engineer's office was in charge of construction.

In connection with this loop-line project eight reinforced concrete road bridges of modern design were also built in the vicinity between 1931 and 1933. Four carry the railway track across roads, and four carry roads across the track.

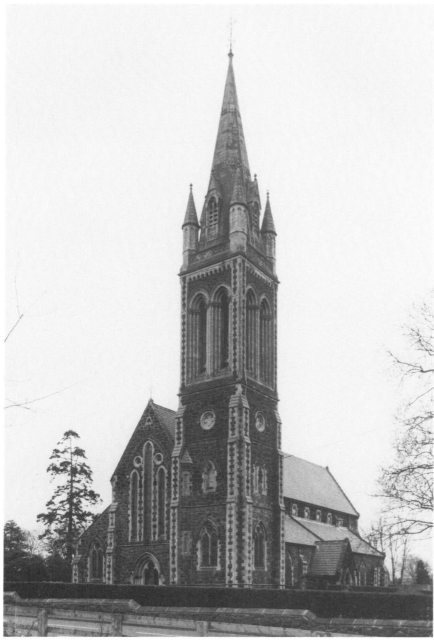

St Mary's Star of the Sea Roman Catholic Church, Whitehouse

Bleach Green Viaduct, Whiteabbey

PLATE XVIII. *Parliament Buildings. The Central Hall. See E4.*

PLATE XIX. *The Royal Courts of Justice. The Central Hall. See 199.*

PLATE XX. *St Bernadette's Roman Catholic Church. Interior. See 235.*

N6 **THE FLORAL HALL**, Belfast Zoological Gardens, Antrim Road.
David W. Boyd, 1935–6 (J. & R. W. Taggart, builders).

A striking and, for Belfast, rare enough example of a particular brand of 1930's modernism. It has a large shallow domed rotunda, smooth white walls, metal windows and a portico of plain columns. Built of concrete blocks cemented and finished white with steel trusses to the auditorium. The original colour scheme inside was blue and gold, with the entrance hall in tangerine. This was a popular place of recreation and entertainment, with concerts, dances and cafes, but has been closed for some years.

The Floral Hall shortly after opening

N7 **WHITEWELL HOUSING ESTATE**, Whitewell Road.
Nothern Ireland Housing Trust Technical Staff, 1947–9.

'The White City', a series of white flat roofed blocks on the slopes of Cavehill, is the earliest of a number of estates built in the Orlit system. It consisted of precast concrete frames with precast concrete floor and roof beams, and exterior walls of precast concrete blocks – a non-traditional system of building which had the advantages of speedy simple erection requiring little skilled labour, and little call for timber.

To the north on Whitewell Road is the former Thronemount Primary School built of Orlit construction between 1953 and 1957. Its multi-leveled flat roofed blocks owe a debt to the Dutchman Dudok.

Whitewell Housing Estate

N8 **MERVILLE GARDEN VILLAGE**, Shore Road, Whitehouse.
E. Prentice Mawson of London, 1947–9 (McGrath Brothers, builders).

The first and best of an ambitious series of housing estates built by Thomas Arlow McGrath, the founder of Ulster Garden Villages Limited. A long narrow site nicely handled with a large block of flats and shops at the entrance and groups of dwellings off a double roadway beyond.

The old 19th century Merville House by Thomas Jackson was retained to serve as a community centre at the lower end of the estate.

Other U.G.V. estates in the vicinity are Abbot's Cross, Fernagh, Prince's Park, and King's Park, all built 1949–50 just before the company's liquidation in 1951.

Merville Garden Village

N9 **ST COMGALL'S CHURCH OF IRELAND**, Carmeen Drive, Rathcoole Estate.
Denis O'D. Hanna, 1955 (F. & W. Bell, builders).

Instead of following the normal but costly practice of erecting two separate buildings, or going for the dubious expedient of a dual-purpose building, Hanna here placed the church directly on top of the hall, an unusual arrangement for the time.

Nearby in Rathmore Drive is Rathcoole Presbyterian Church by Robert McKinstry, 1957, a dual purpose pitched roofed hall with a glazed tower.

St Comgall's Church of Ireland, Rathcoole

Drumbo Round Tower

S1 **THE GIANT'S RING**, off Ballyles-son Road, Ballynahatty townland, in the Parish of Drumbo.

Of uncertain date and function, the Giant's Ring may possibly be a late Neolithic ceremonial or assembly site. It consists of a circular space about 580 feet diameter enclosed by an earthen mound. Near the centre is a chambered grave traditionally known as a cromlech, an arrangement of five stone uprights with a large capstone, fancifully referred to at one time as a "druidical altar".

S2 **DRUMBO ROUND TOWER**, in the Presbyterian churchyard, Drumbo.

Only a stump of an Irish Round Tower but the nearest example to Belfast of the most singular building type of the Early Christian Irish. Tall conically capped tapering circular towers with elevated doorway were built all over Ireland from the 9th to 12th centuries as belfries (for the ringing of hand bells) and as monastic keeps.

This distinctive form of belfry was taken up by 19th century architects indulging in Irish revivalism.

S3 **SHAW'S BRIDGE**, Malone Road. 1709.

A ford over the Lagan was bridged here by Captain Shaw of Cromwell's army. His timber bridge was later replaced by one of stone in 1698 but it was destroyed by flood and rebuilt in 1709. What stands here now is thus basically of late 17th or early 18th century date. Recently bypassed by a modern road and bridge.

The Giant's Ring, Drumbo: early nineteenth century engraving of the cromlech

Shaw's Bridge

S4 KNOCKBREDA PARISH CHURCH (Church of Ireland), Church Road, Newtownbreda.
Richard Castle of Dublin, 1737.

Designed by the leading architect in Ireland at the time, Richard Castle or Cassels as he is sometimes referred, this church was built by the Dowager Viscountess Middleton at her sole expense. Her offer of a church was made and accepted in 1733 and the completed building consecrated in August 1737 (not 1747 as so often reported). Its tidy plan and crisp classical detailing moved Harris to describe it in 1744 in the *Antient and Present State of the County of Down* as "a building the neatest and most compleat perhaps of this kind in the kingdom."

The apsidal chancel was added by Thomas Drew in 1883; the vestry by R. I. Calwell CE, in 1910.

In the churchyard are some fine monuments. The most important are three large late 18th century classical mausoleums, square-plan with corner columns and ogee domed roofs. These are the Rainey Memorial of probably *c.*1790, the larger Cunningham Memorial of *c.*1797, and the magnificent Greg Memorial of *c.*1796. No architect's name is recorded but the style is a blend of Chambers and Gibbs, possibly based on some of their published designs for pavilions and small temples. A fourth example of the type here, with illegible inscription, was demolished in the over-zealous tidying of the churchyard in 1986.

19th century monuments to note are three Gothic Revival slabs: the Lanyon Family Memorial of *c.*1858, the Riddel Memorial of *c.*1862, and the Fitzpatrick Memorial to a design originally carried out by W. J. Barre in 1865 for the Ferguson Memorial at Balmoral Cemetery, Stockman's Lane.

Knockbreda Parish Church and Churchyard, with the Greg Mausoleum to the right

Knockbreda Churchyard: Fitzpatrick Memorial

Knockbreda Parish Church

Drumbridge Lock-Keeper's House

S5 **DRUMBRIDGE LOCK-KEEPER'S HOUSE**, Upper Malone Road, Drumbeg. **Thomas Omer**, *c*.1759.

Of a number of identical lock-keepers' houses built along the River Lagan to the designs of the Canal Engineer, there remains only this one at Drumbeg and a ruined shell at Ballyskeagh, further up river. It is a neat little design showing how a classical approach could enoble even the most modest of dwellings. An ill-placed plaque informs us that it was restored in 1983.

Malone House, Barnett's Park

S6 **MALONE HOUSE**, Barnett's Park, Malone Road.
Late 1820s; rebuilt by McKinstry and Brown, 1980–2.

The late Georgian house which was bombed and burnt in 1976 was carefully rebuilt in 1980–2 with as much as possible of the original re-instated. An interesting departure, however, is the introduction in the large bowed room of decorative plasterwork cast from moulds taken directly from the derelict 18th century Mount Panther house near Clough, Co. Down. Malone House was presented to the city in 1946 and is open to the public.

The gatelodge on Malone Road, was by Blackwood and Jury, 1921.

Wilmont House, Sir Thomas and Lady Dixon Park

S7 **WILMONT HOUSE**, Sir Thomas and Lady Dixon Park, Upper Malone Road. **Thomas Jackson**, 1859.

A large but plain mid-Victorian house originally a double mansion, or large semi-detached building, that was later united in one dwelling. Built for James Bristow, Chairman of the Northern Bank, and for his son. The house has been an old people's home since 1963, and the grounds open to the public as a park.

S8 HOLY TRINITY CHURCH OF IRELAND, Ballylesson Road, Drumbo. **Welland and Gillespie** of Dublin, 1863–4, incorporating a tower of 1789–90.

On a hill top site not far from the Giant's Ring, Drumbo Parish Church consists of an old pinnacled tower together with a nave, chancel and transepts in the standard Gothic Revival style of the architects to the Board of Ecclesiastical Commissioners. It has their typical bold plate traceried rose windows.

In the churchyard is a large mausoleum to the Batt family, a rectangular block with a pedestal, column and urn, dating from the 1840s.

Holy Trinity Church of Ireland, Drumbo

S9 ST PATRICK'S CHURCH OF IRELAND, Drumbridge, Drumbeg. **Thomas Drew**, 1868–70.

Of the original 18th century church only the west tower (with its rebuilt spire of 1833) and part of the west wall of the nave remains. The main body of the church was rebuilt by the Gothic Revivalist Drew who also added the lychgate in 1878.

In the churchyard are a number of mainly 19th century memorials. Among the more architecturally interesting are the McCance Memorial slab of 1827 with Regency Greek detailing; the Hill Charley Memorial slab, of uncertain date but in late Georgian Tudor Revivalist style; the Bristow Memorials, the Weir Memorial, and the Matthew Charley Memorial, all Gothic slabs of the 1860s, the latter with Lanyon and Lynn's characteristic Early English detailing. There is also a fine Celtic Cross to Walter Henry Wilson of 1904, carved by O'Dwyer of Kilkenny.

St Patrick's Church of Ireland, Drumbeg

S10 RATHMORE, Kingsway, Finaghy. Probably by **Lanyon, Lynn and Lanyon**, 1870.

A substantial mid-Victorian house built of sandstone. Italianate in style with Tuscan columned porch and a very impressive coffer-vaulted hall with coloured rooflight and Corinthian colonnade. Built for Victor Coates, iron founder; now a convent and school. There are similarities with Stradbally Hall, Co. Leix, and Newtownbarry House, Co. Wexford, both by Lanyon, Lynn and Lanyon.

Rathmore, Finaghy

S11 **BELVOIR PARK HOSPITAL**, Hospital Road, Purdysburn.
Young and Mackenzie, 1904–6.

Built as the Infectious Diseases Hospital, this is a range of fairly plain red brick buildings but enlivened by English classical detailing around the entrance bays. Stone carving by Winter & Thompson; patent electric turret clock by Sharman D. Neill.

Belvoir Park Hospital

E1 **CASTLEREAGH PRESBYTERIAN CHURCH**, Church Road, Castlereagh.
John Miller, 1834–5.

A distinguished stuccoed Neo-classical church with an Ionic *in antis* porch. Its columns have distinctive capitals and wide flaring bases derived from the Greek temple at Bassae. Its crowning feature, a monopteral tempietto derived from the Monument of Lysicrates in Athens, is reputedly the first instance of a belfry on a Presbyterian church in Ireland. A very fine galleried interior.

Castlereagh Presbyterian Church

E2 **CLELAND MAUSOLEUM**, St. Elizabeth's Churchyard, Dundonald.
1842.

Erected to the memory of Samuel Cleland of Storm Mount (a house later enlarged to become Stormont Castle) this dramatically sited Neo-classical monument is one of the largest mausoleums in Ulster. An impressively stacked Greek Revival pile, it consists of a large cubic core with Doric columns and pediments bedecked with acroteria and urns, surmounted by a Lysicratic cuploa in Ionic style.

To the east of the churchyard is the rather naive Gothic stuccoed Dundonald Presbyterian Church, originally built 1839–9 but much enlarged by James Entwhistle, 1858–9. The Tudoresque school in freestone was opened in 1844.

Cleland Mausoleum, Dundonald

E3 **STORMONT CASTLE**, Upper Newtownards Road.
Thomas Turner, 1858 (John Lowry, builder).

A striking towered and turreted composition in Scrabo sandstone. With its rather Scottish style corbelled bartizans and Irish looking crenellated parapets, Stormont Castle was an extensive enlargment of an earlier and plainer house on the site. The Scottish Baronial style of this transformation was appropriate enough as the Clelands of Storm Mount (as the house of 1830 was called) were descended from an old Lanarkshire family. As so often the case with such 'castles' the interiors were carried out in classical style. At one time the official residence of the Prime Minister of Northern Ireland, it is now used as government offices.

In the garden beside the house is a Gothick conservatory of the later 1830s.

Stormont Castle at the turn of the century

Stormont Castle: interior of saloon in 1894

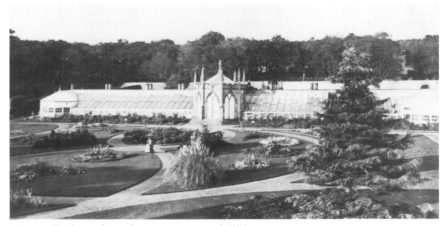

Stormont Castle: garden and conservatory around 1894

Parliament Buildings: the portico

E4 PARLIAMENT BUILDINGS,
Upper Newtownards Road, Stormont.
Arnold Thornley of Liverpool, 1927–32
(Stewart & Partners, builders).

One of the most outstanding architectural sights in Ireland, Parliament Buildings enjoys a magnificent and commmanding situation to the east of the city. Distant views of it are particularly fine and impressive. It lies at the top of a broad processional avenue which rises gradually for three quarters of a mile from the main road and culminates in a flight of approach steps 90 feet wide.

The building has a very dignified exterior and a well laid out axial plan. Built of masonry construction in Portland stone on a plinth of unpolished Mourne granite it is designed in a Neo-classical style which is fairly plain in treatment except around the three entrance bays. Elaborate central feature to main facade with a wealth of Greek detail and a grand Ionic temple front. Pediment carved with a group showing 'Ulster bearing the Golden Flame of Loyalty to the Crown', carved by Malcolm Miller and Rendal Bond of Earp, Hobbs and Miller of Manchester. The portico and entrance hall lead to the main feature of the interior, the Central Hall, with its splendidly coloured ceiling, walls faced in Travertine marble, and a bronze balustraded marble staircase leading to the galleries around it. On the first landing is a bronze statue by Leonard S. Merrifield of James Craig, first Viscount Craigavon of Stormont and first Prime Minister of Northern Ireland, unveiled in 1945. Off to each side of the Central Hall, through circular lobbies, lie the old Commons Chamber to the west and Senate Chamber to the east. Much of the rest of the accommodation was given over to offices as it was built as both a Parliament House and an executive building.

Large though the building is, it is in fact a great deal smaller than first projected. It was originally intended in 1922 that Thornley would be architect for the Houses of Parliament and Ralph Knott of London would be architect for two blocks of administrative buildings to flank it at right angles. Plans were prepared by 1923 and foundations laid for a great domed Parliament House before the scheme was curtailed. Thornley then had the task of designing a new combined block to be built on the foundation already laid. This final design was prepared by 1927 and the foundation stone of the building was laid the following year.

In the grounds to the right of the building is the tomb of Lord Craigavon, a large block of dressed Portland stone designed by R. Ingleby Smith who did not live to see it finished in 1942.

In front of the building stands the statue of Lord Carson by Merrifield, unveiled 1934.

Fine entrance gateways to Upper Newtownards Road and to Massey Avenue together with dainty little Portland stone porters' lodges designed by Thornley.

The arrangement of avenues and the general layout of the grounds was also designed by Thornley. Following the completion of the whole project he was knighted in 1932, and in 1933 Parliament Buildings was awarded the RIBA Ulster Architecture Medal.

Behind the trees to the east, down hill from Parliament Buildings and not visible to the public, is the red brick Neo-Georgian **Speaker's House** by Knott and Collins of London, 1926.

Outside the Massey Avenue entrance gateway is the Neo-Georgian former Provincial Bank, in Portland stone and Westmorland slates by Thornley , 1932 (Stewart & Partners, builders).

See pl. XVIII.

Parliament Buildings, Stormont

Parliament Buildings: front gateway and lodge

The Speaker's House, Stormont

E5 STORMONT PRESBYTERIAN CHURCH, Upper Newtownards Road. Thomas T. Houston, 1950–5.

The round arched work of Thomas J. Houston's church hall of 1930–1 set the tone for his son's post-war church. Plain Romanesque in reconstructed stone. A Byzantinesque dome was designed for the tower but not carried out. Airy and modern interior. Stone font with figured reliefs, carved by Rosamond Praeger.

Another plain round arched Presbyterian church of the time is that on Crumlin Road, by D. W. Boyd, 1952, carried out in rustic brick.

E6 ST MOLUA'S CHURCH OF IRELAND, Upper Newtownards Road. Denis O'D. Hanna, 1961–2.

A big hall church in a mixed style with something of Coventry Cathedral in the serrated side windows. Amazingly tall and thin slated finials and spire of oriental or Slavic inspiration. Stone plaques on exterior walls by David Pettigrew. A chain of angels is depicted across the front of the building, symbolic of the protection of Heaven. Inside, a mural of 'The Son of Man', painted by Desmond Kinney.

Church hall to rear also by Hanna, 1961, with a large abstract bronze by James McKendrie.

St Molua's Church of Ireland

E7 DUNDONALD HOUSE, Upper Newtownards Road, Dundonald. Gibson and Taylor, 1963.

One of the first big modern blocks in Ulster. Fussy fenestration but good massing overall with two overlapping blocks of different heights, built on an open site.

Stormont Presbyterian Church

Dundonald House

Index of Architects and Engineers

Numbers relate to entries

Place of practice, Belfast,
except where stated otherwise

Index of Artists and Craftsmen

Numbers relate to entries

Place of practice, Belfast, except where stated otherwise

Index of Buildings and Streets

Numbers relate to entries

Localities and names of streets are given in capitals for use as a topographical guide